Russian Dolls Coloring Book

This Russian Doll Coloring book belongs to:

_____

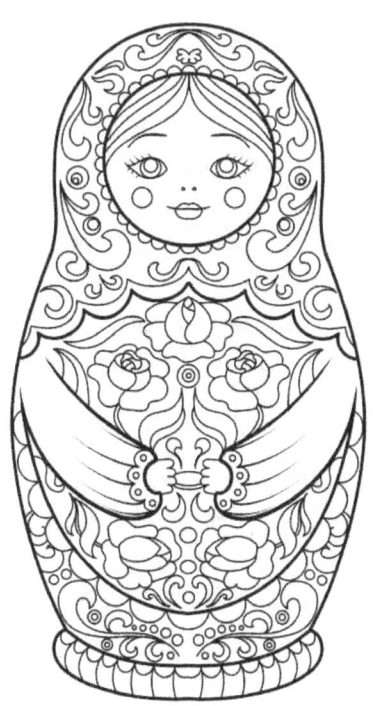

Copyright © 2017 Adult Coloring Books

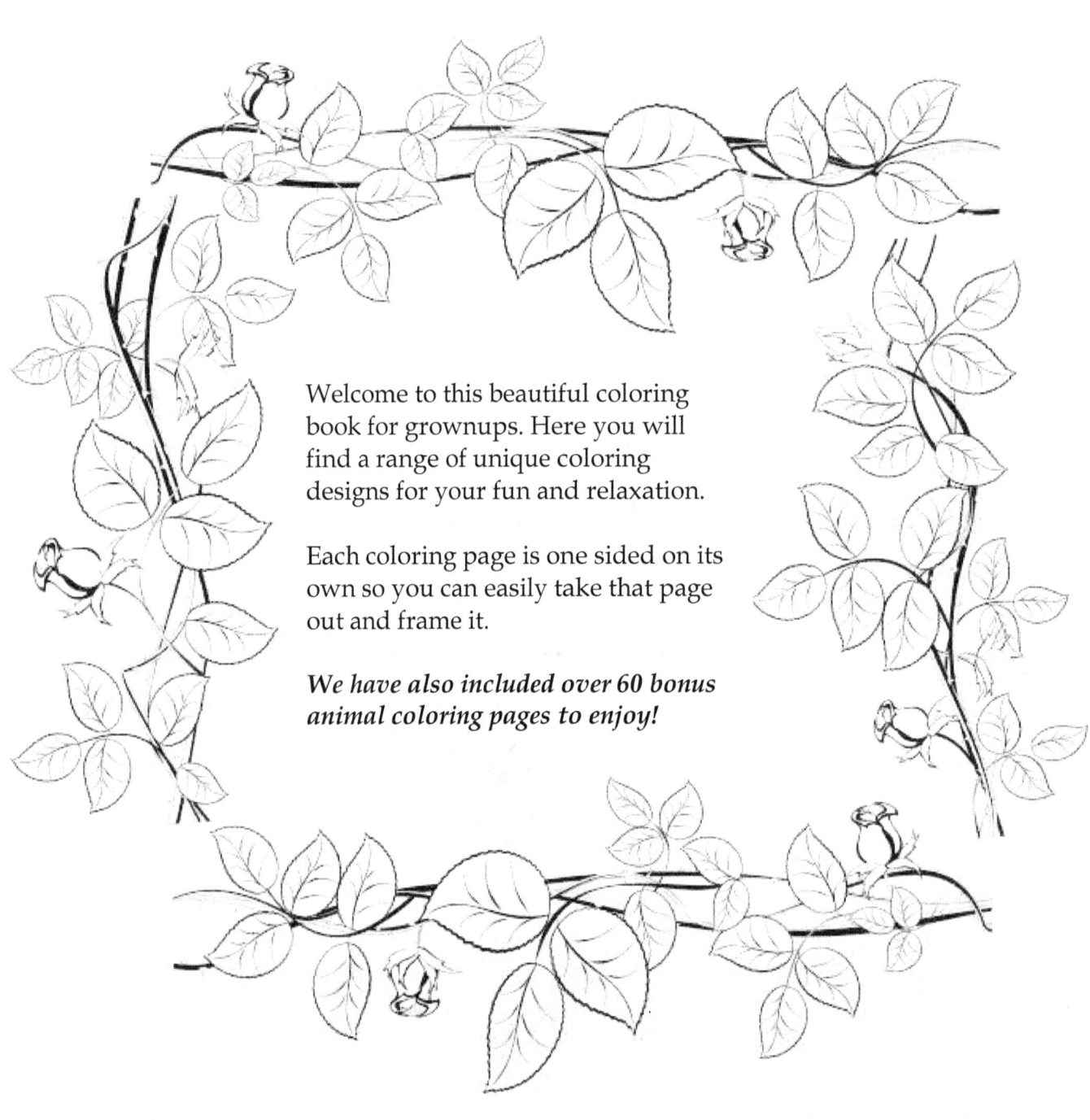

Welcome to this beautiful coloring book for grownups. Here you will find a range of unique coloring designs for your fun and relaxation.

Each coloring page is one sided on its own so you can easily take that page out and frame it.

We have also included over 60 bonus animal coloring pages to enjoy!

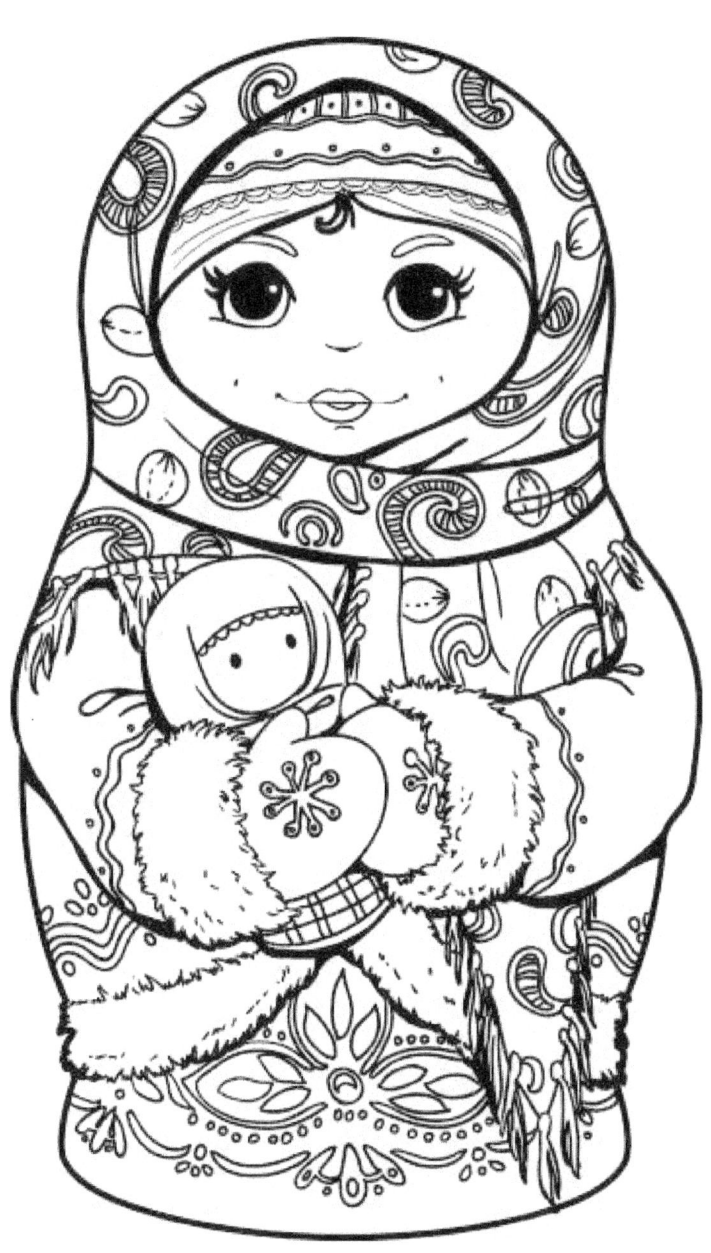

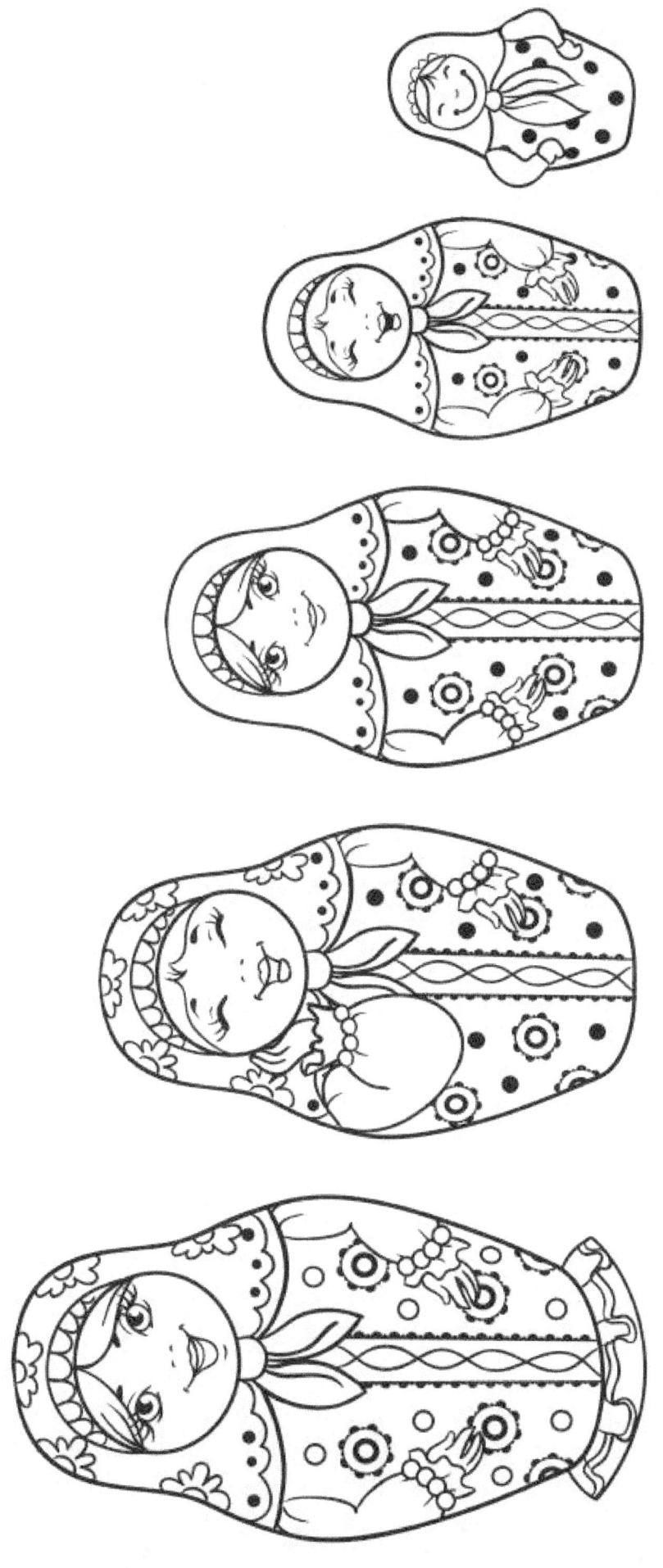

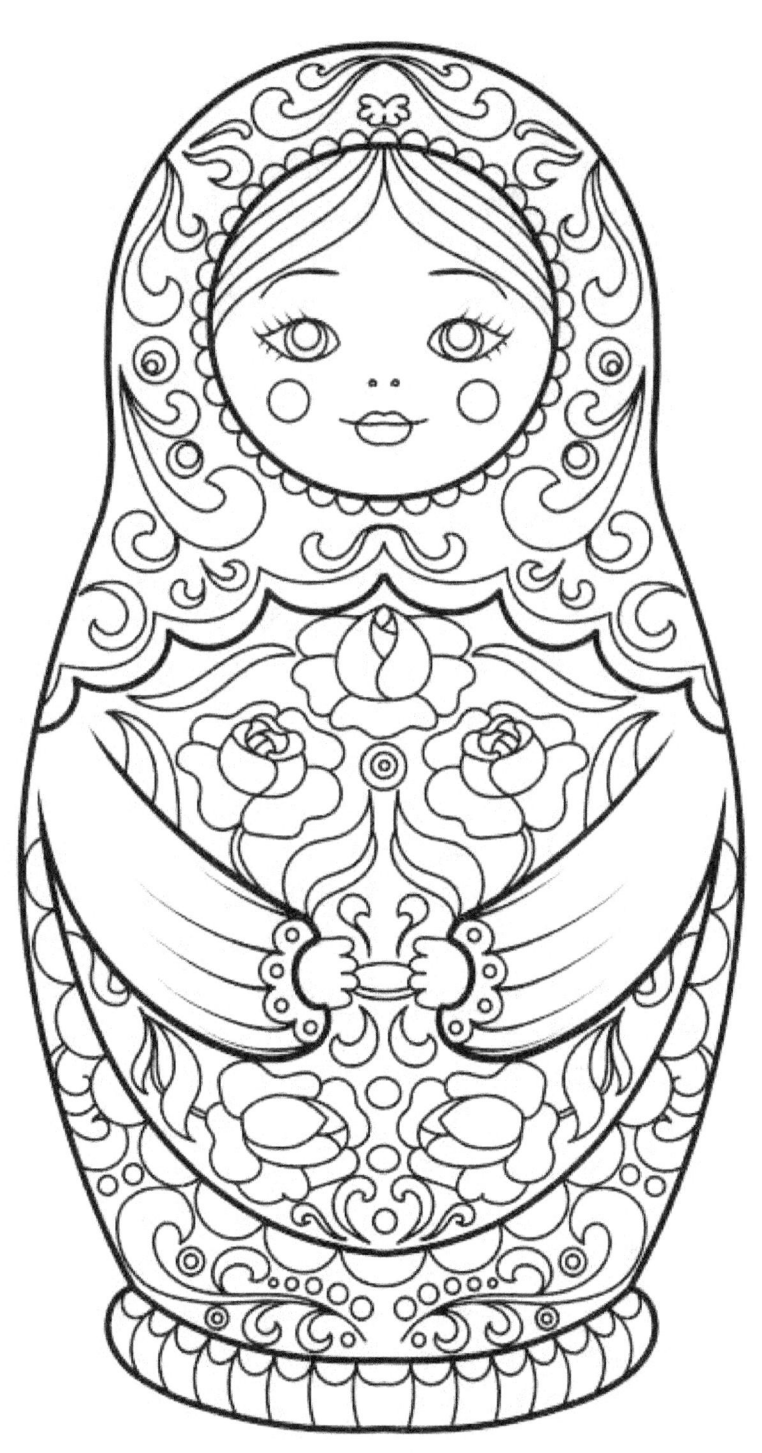

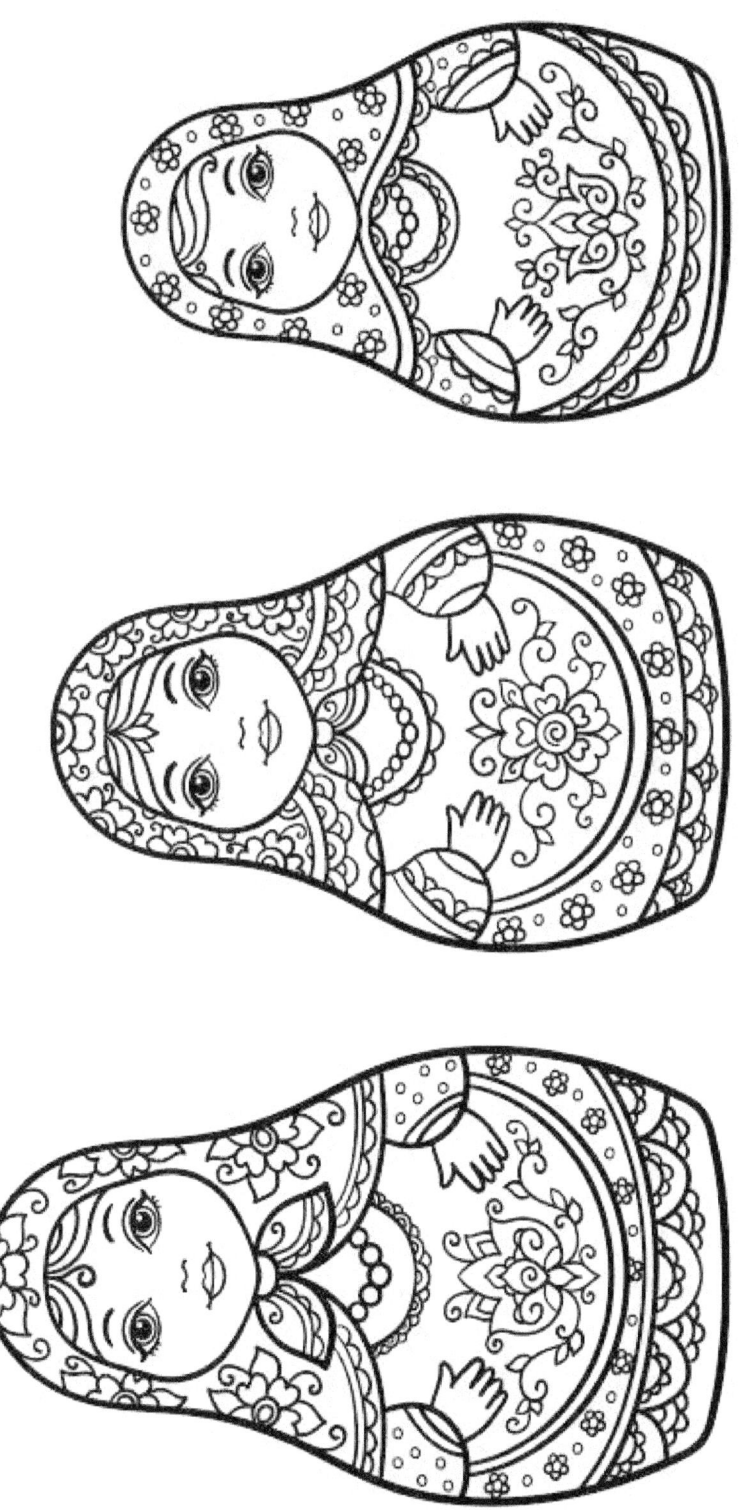

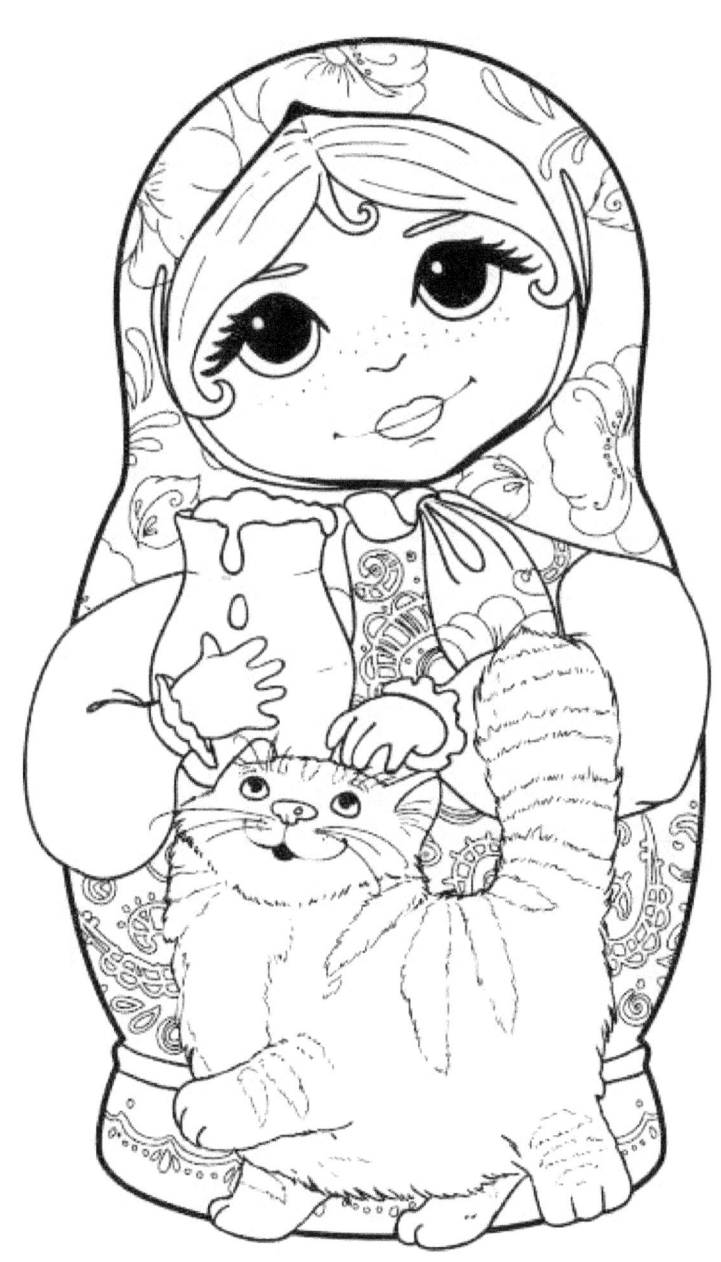

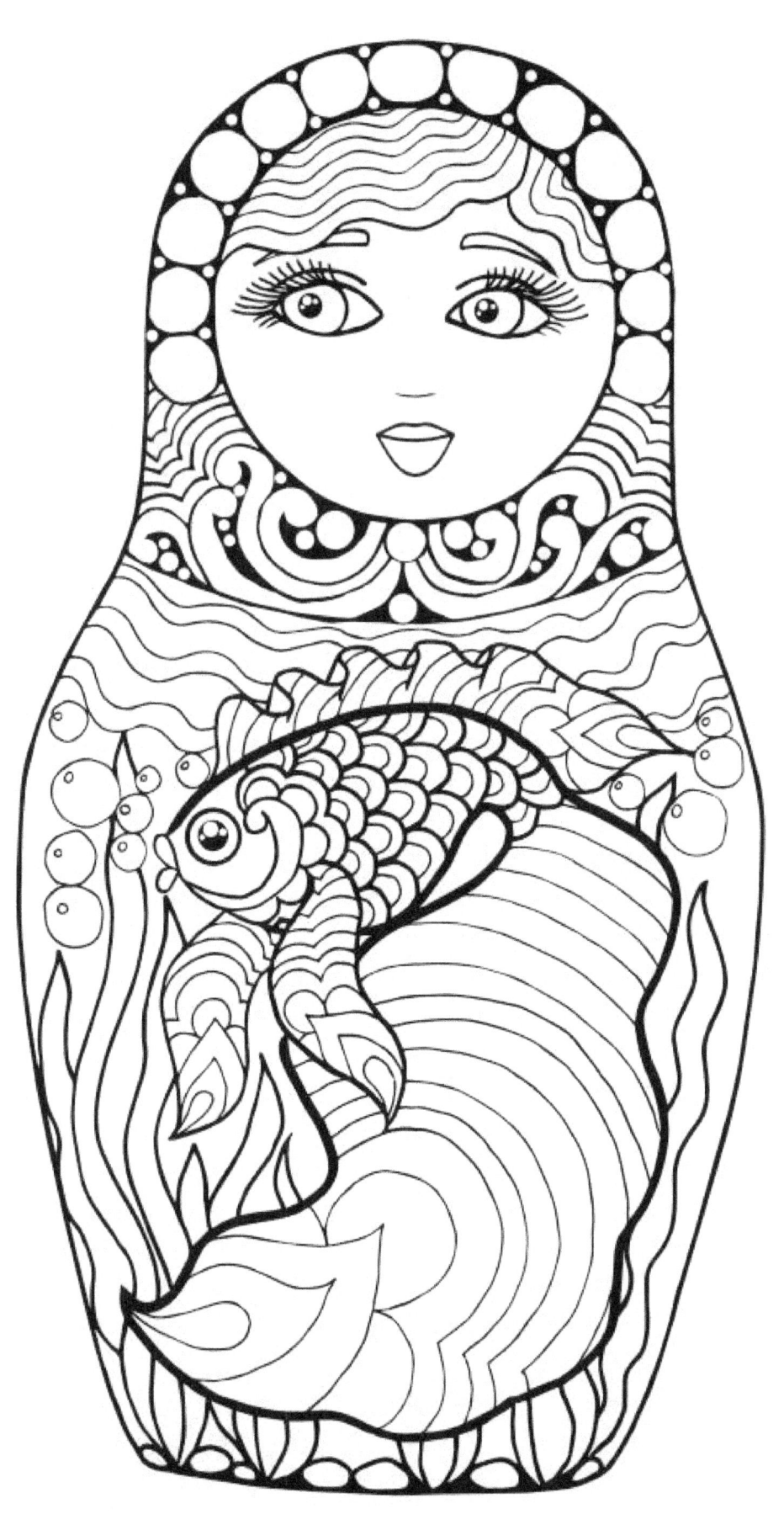

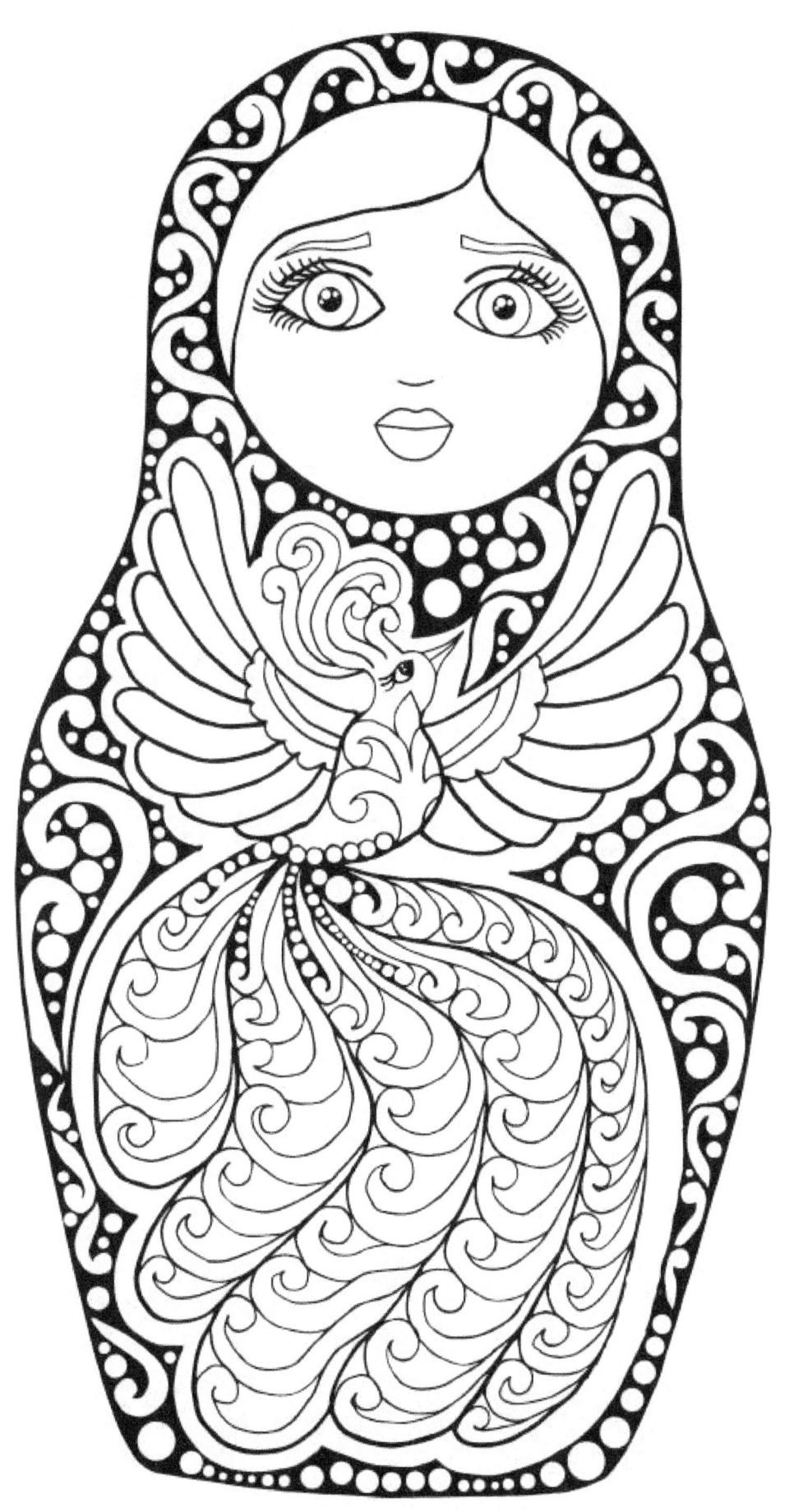

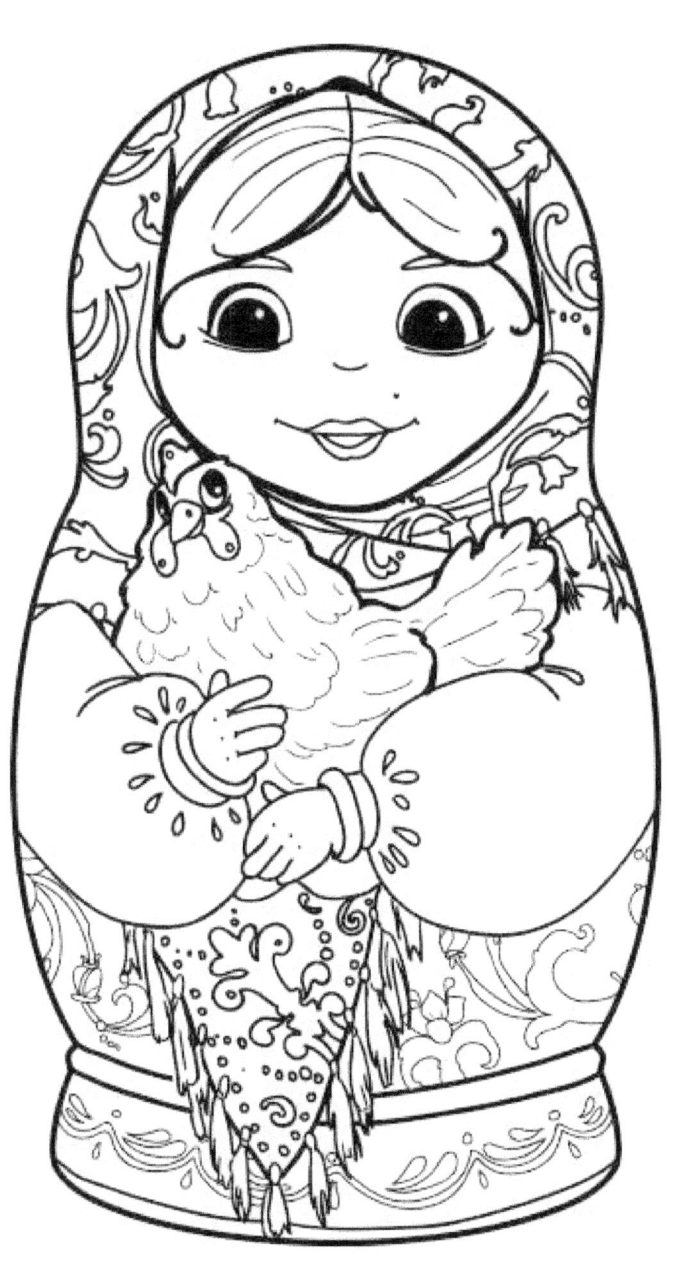

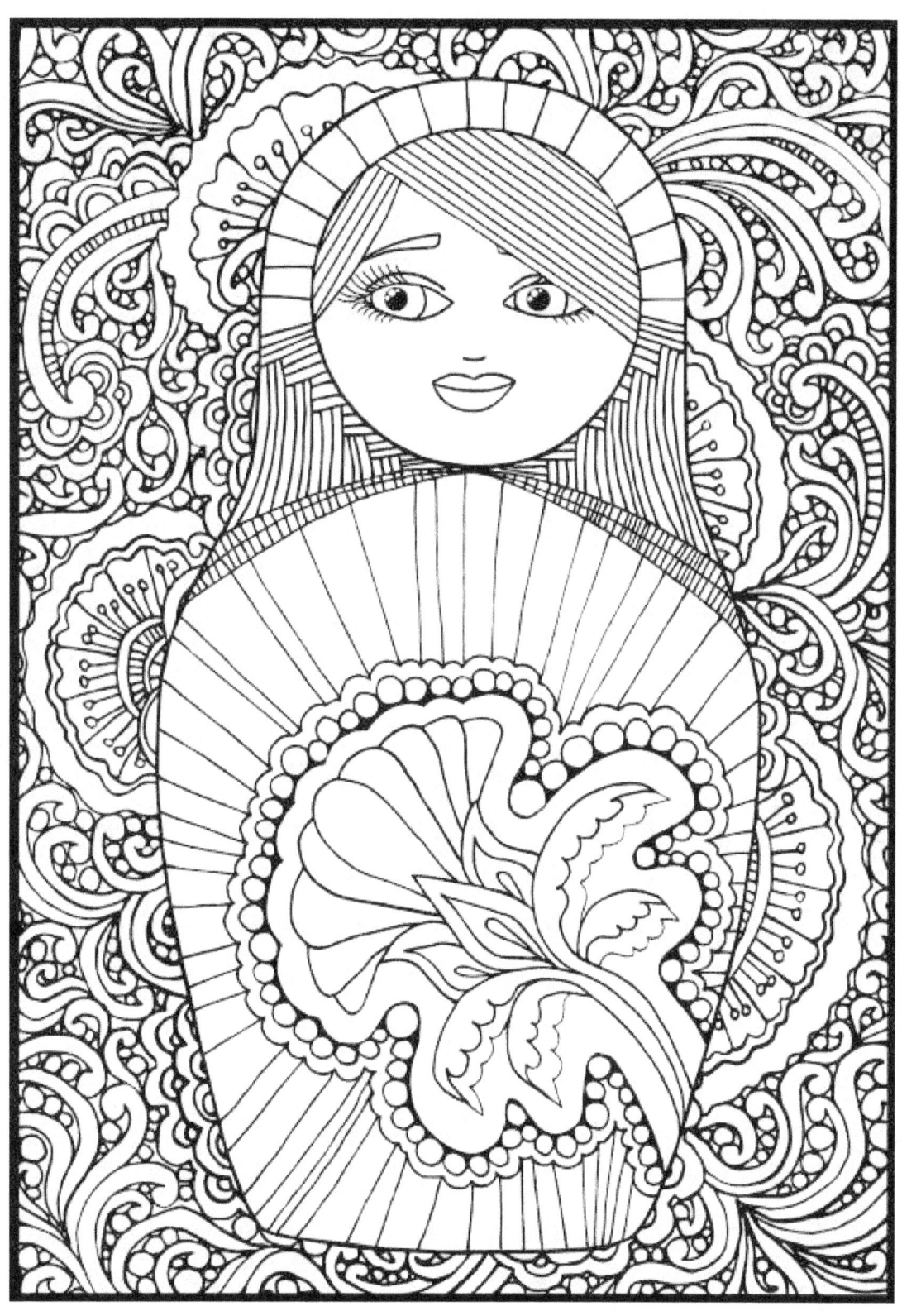

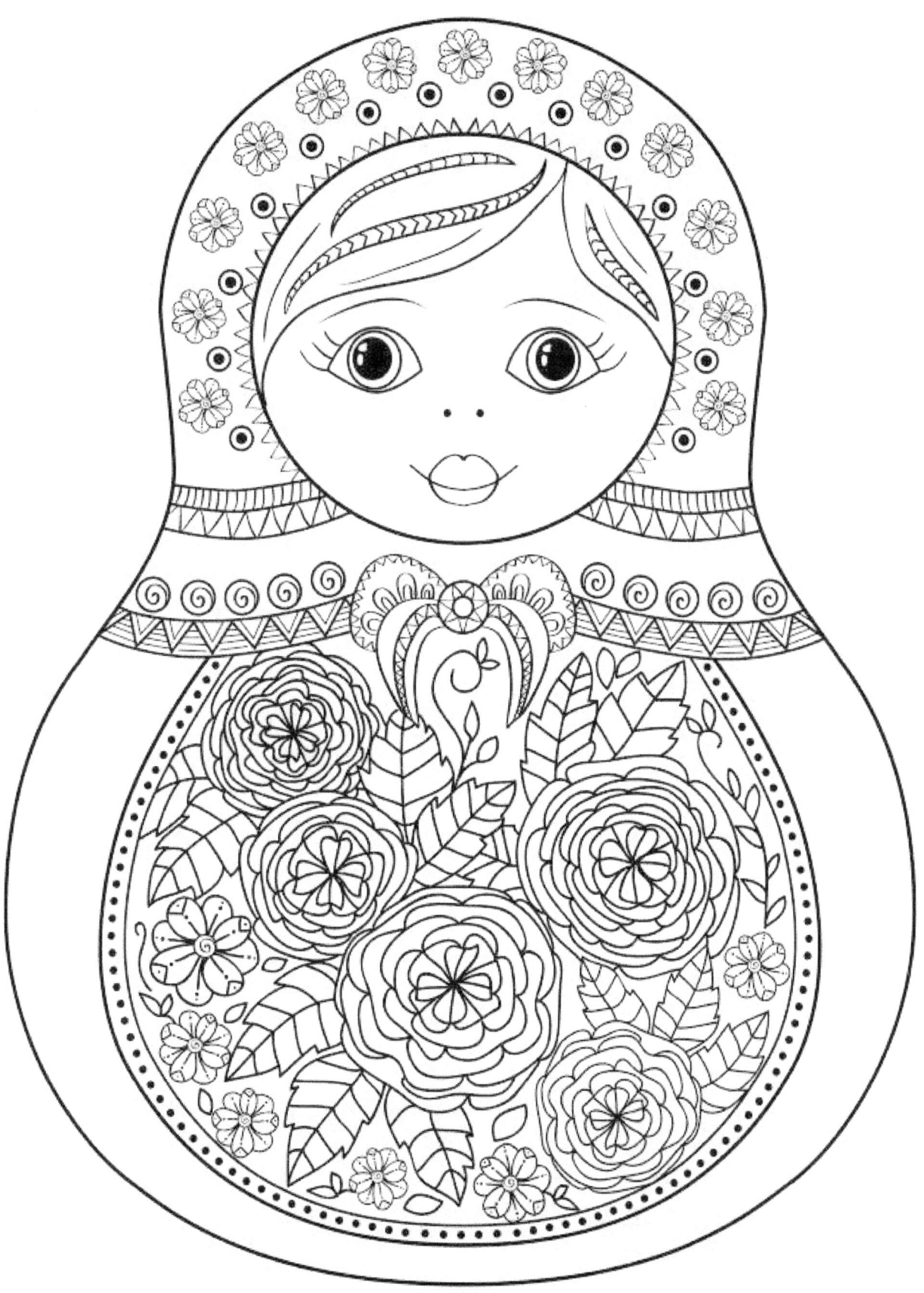

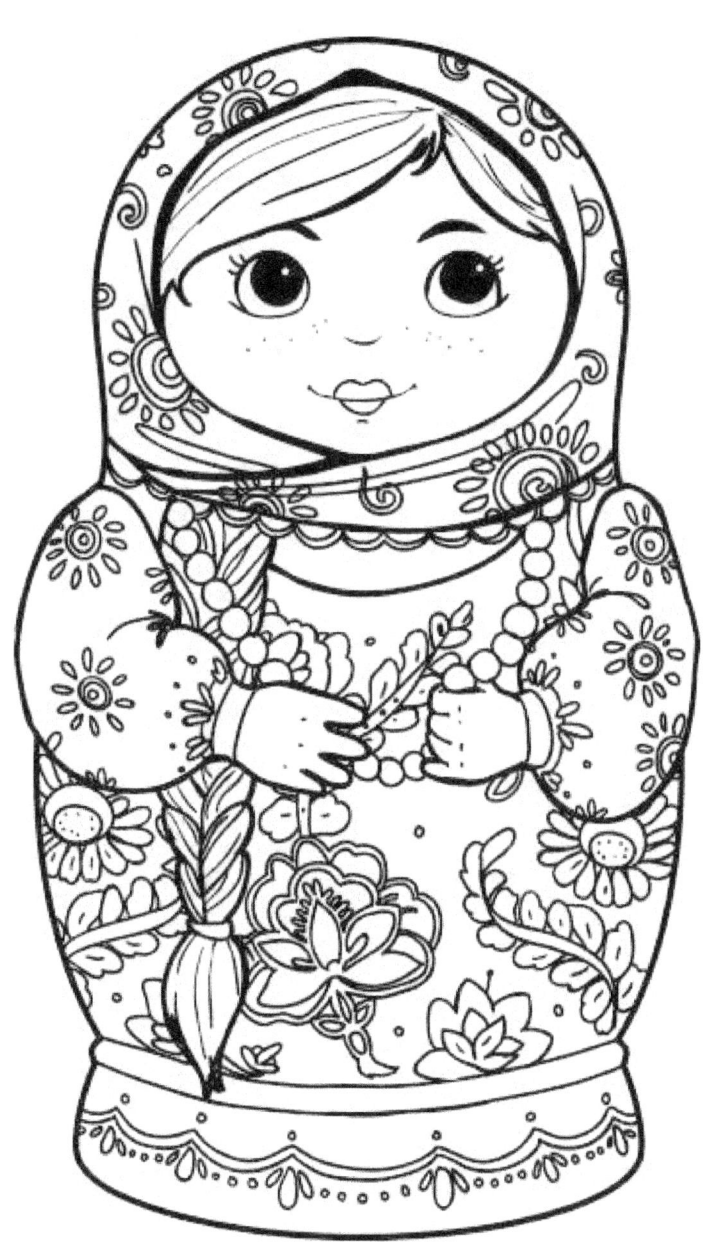

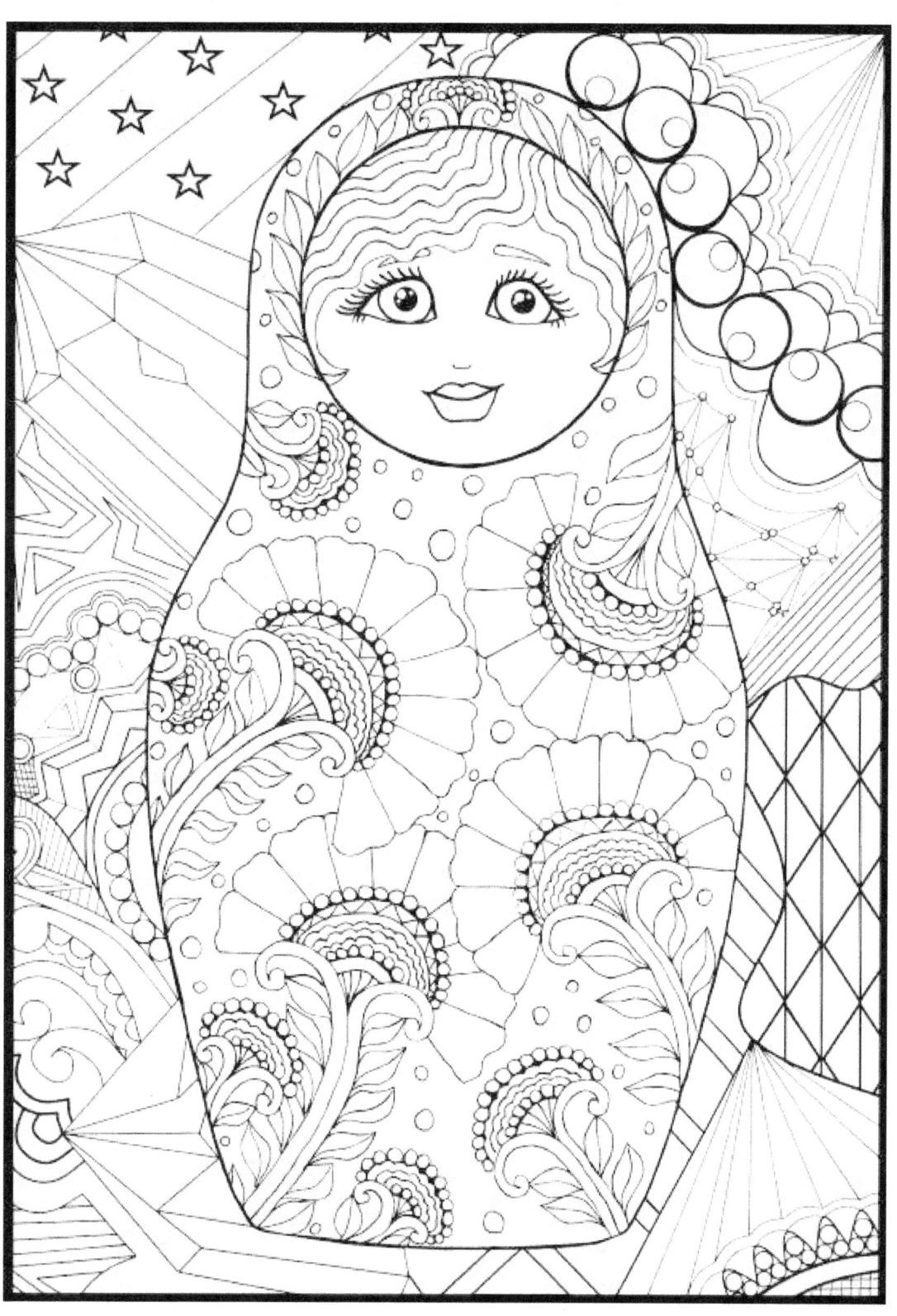

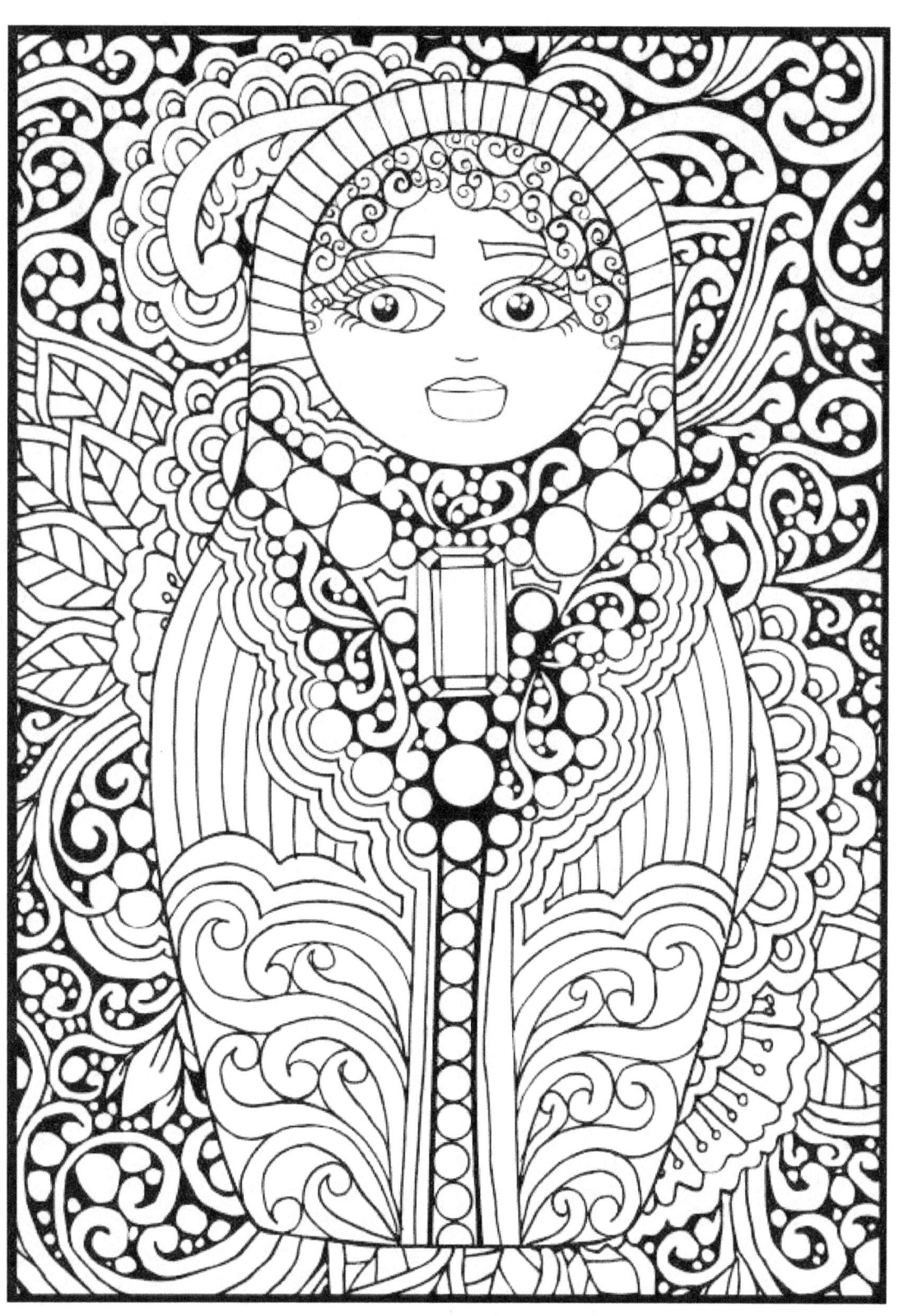

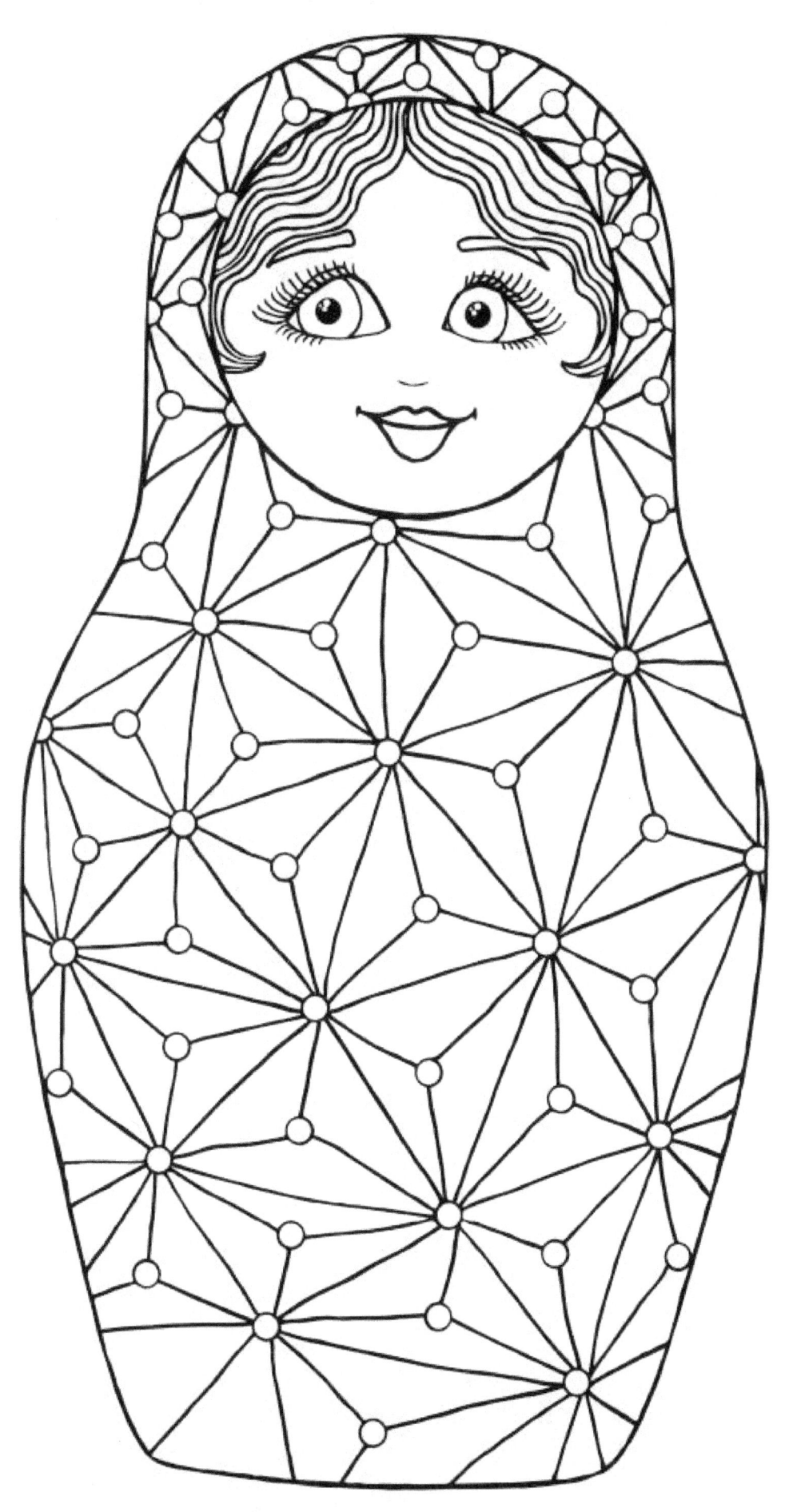

Bonus Animal Coloring Pages as A Special Thank You For Our Loyal Color Fans.

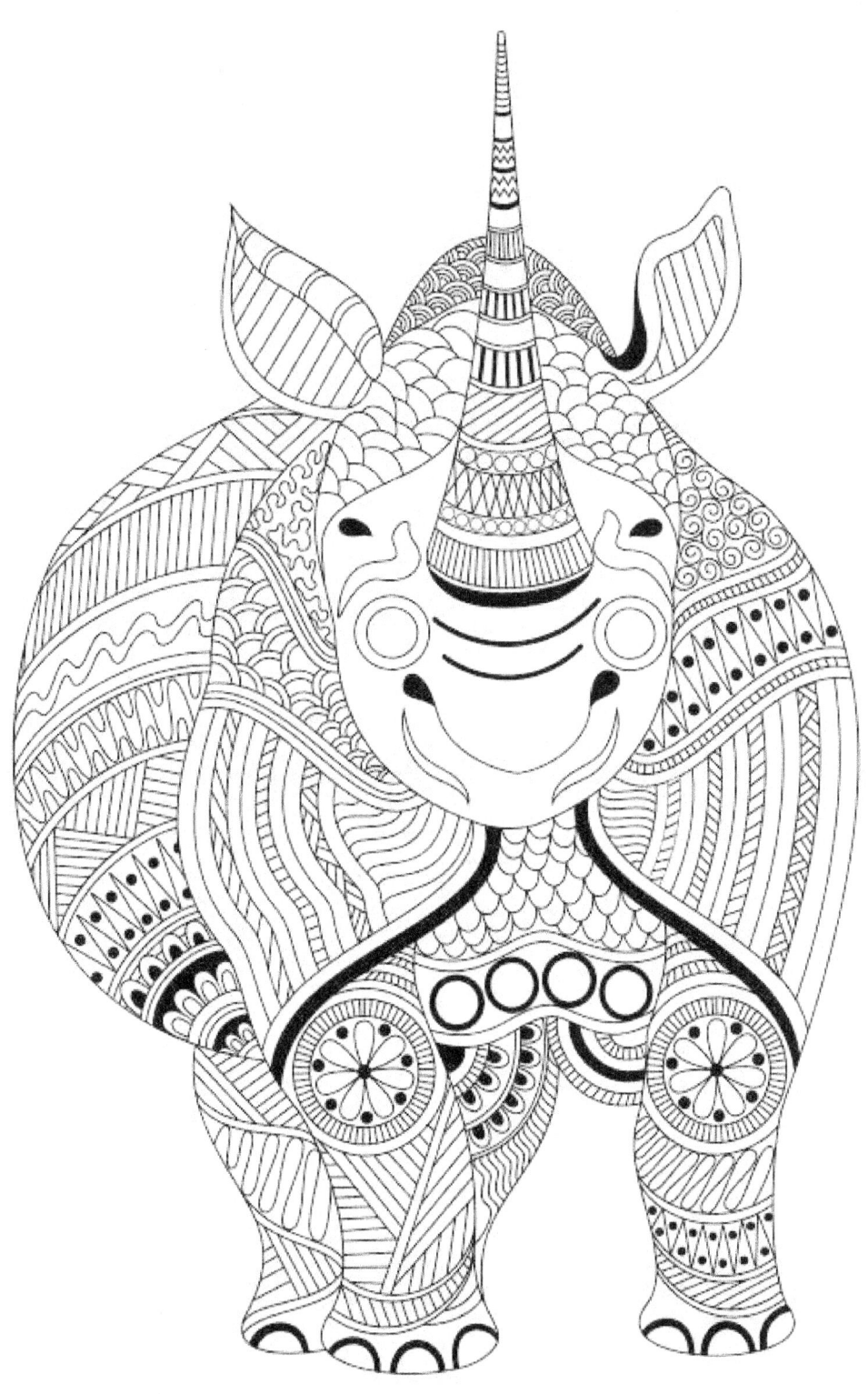

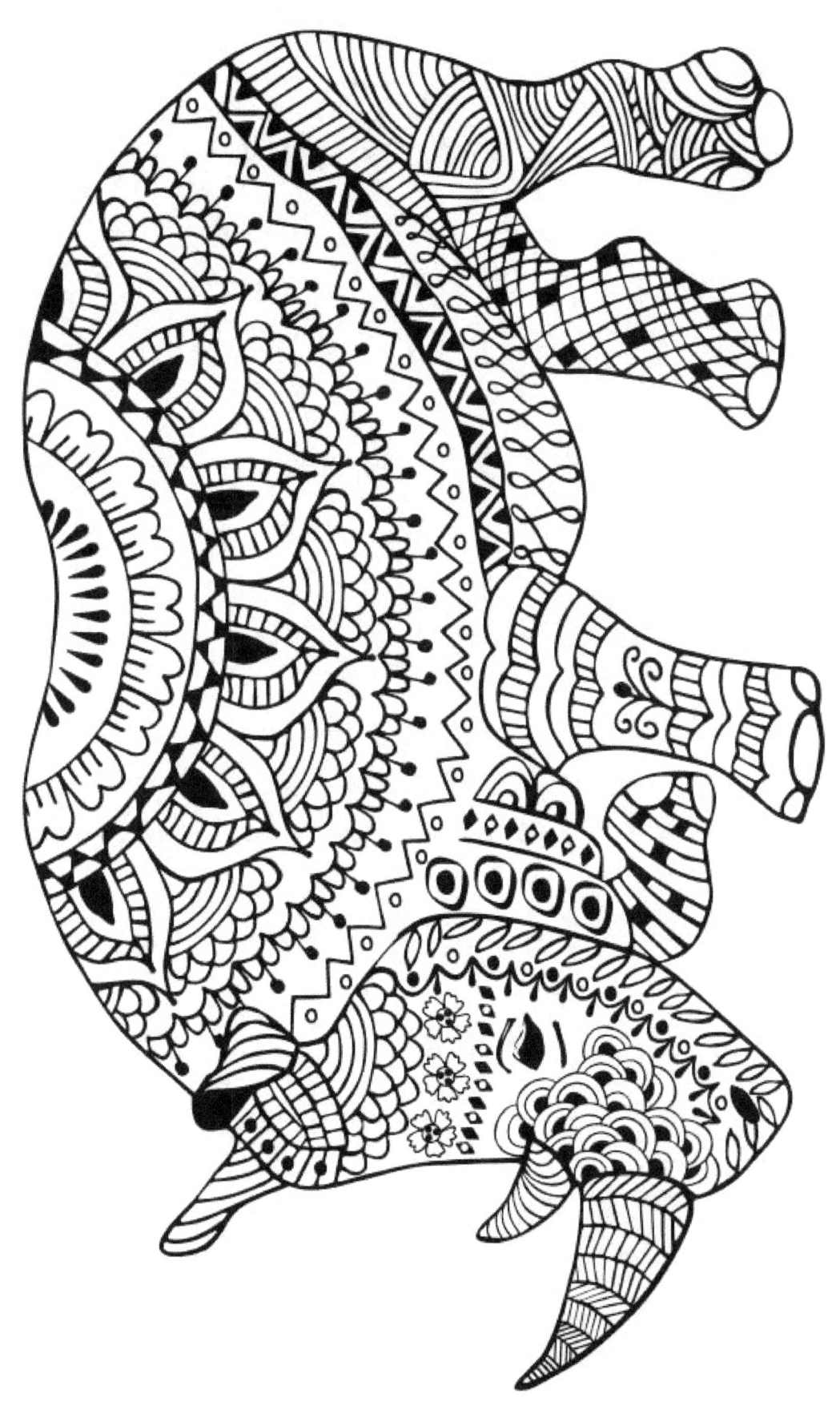

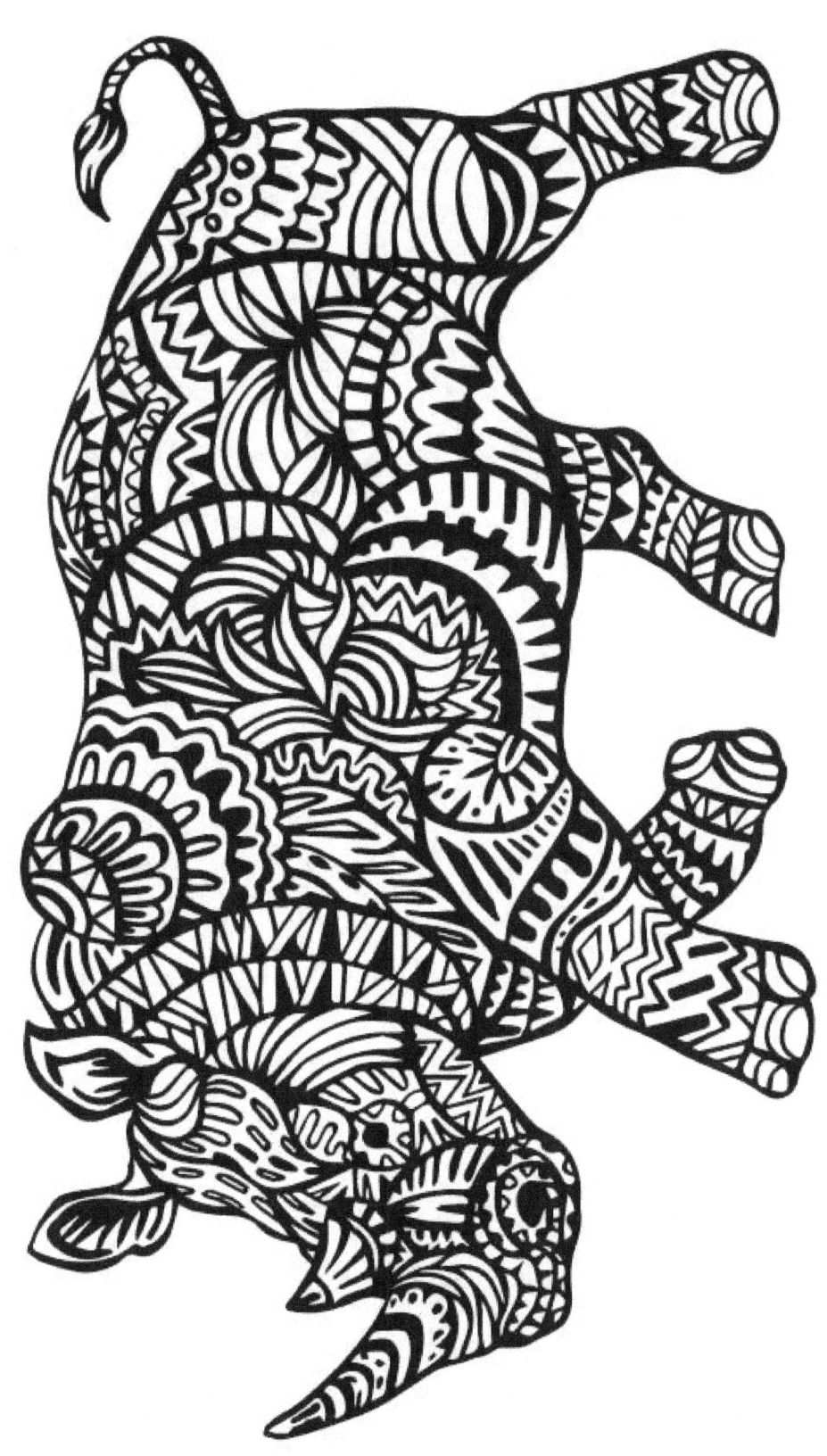

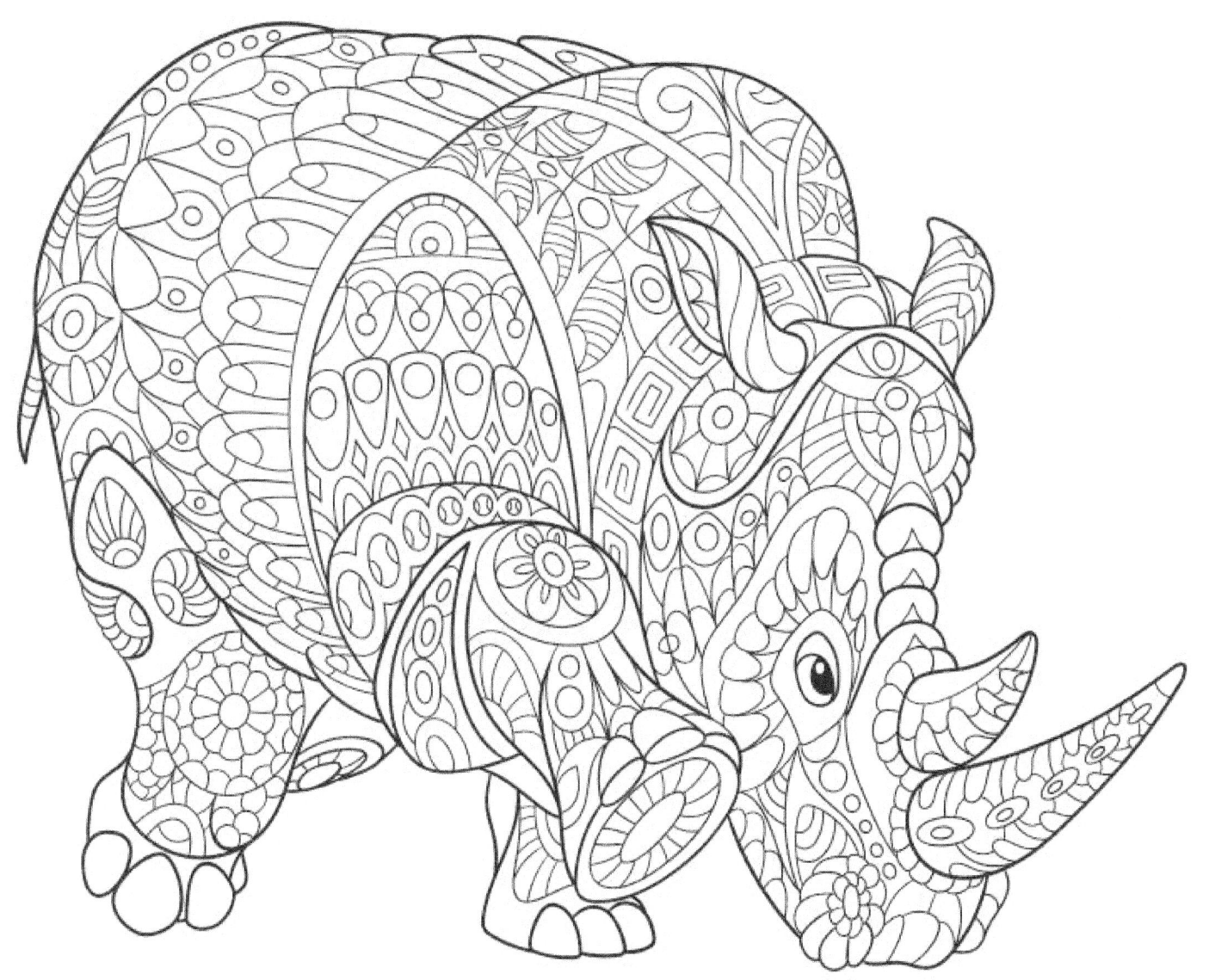

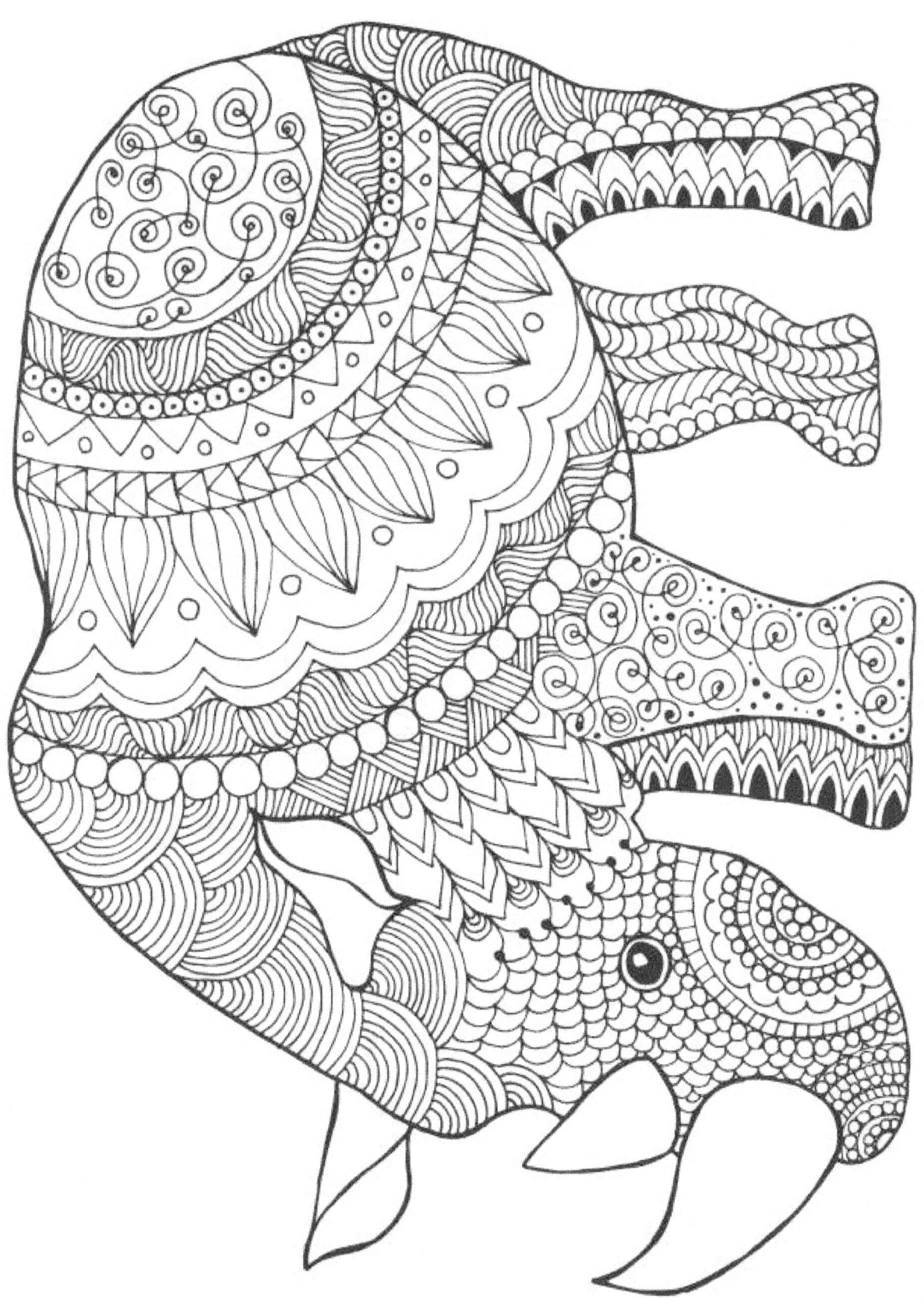

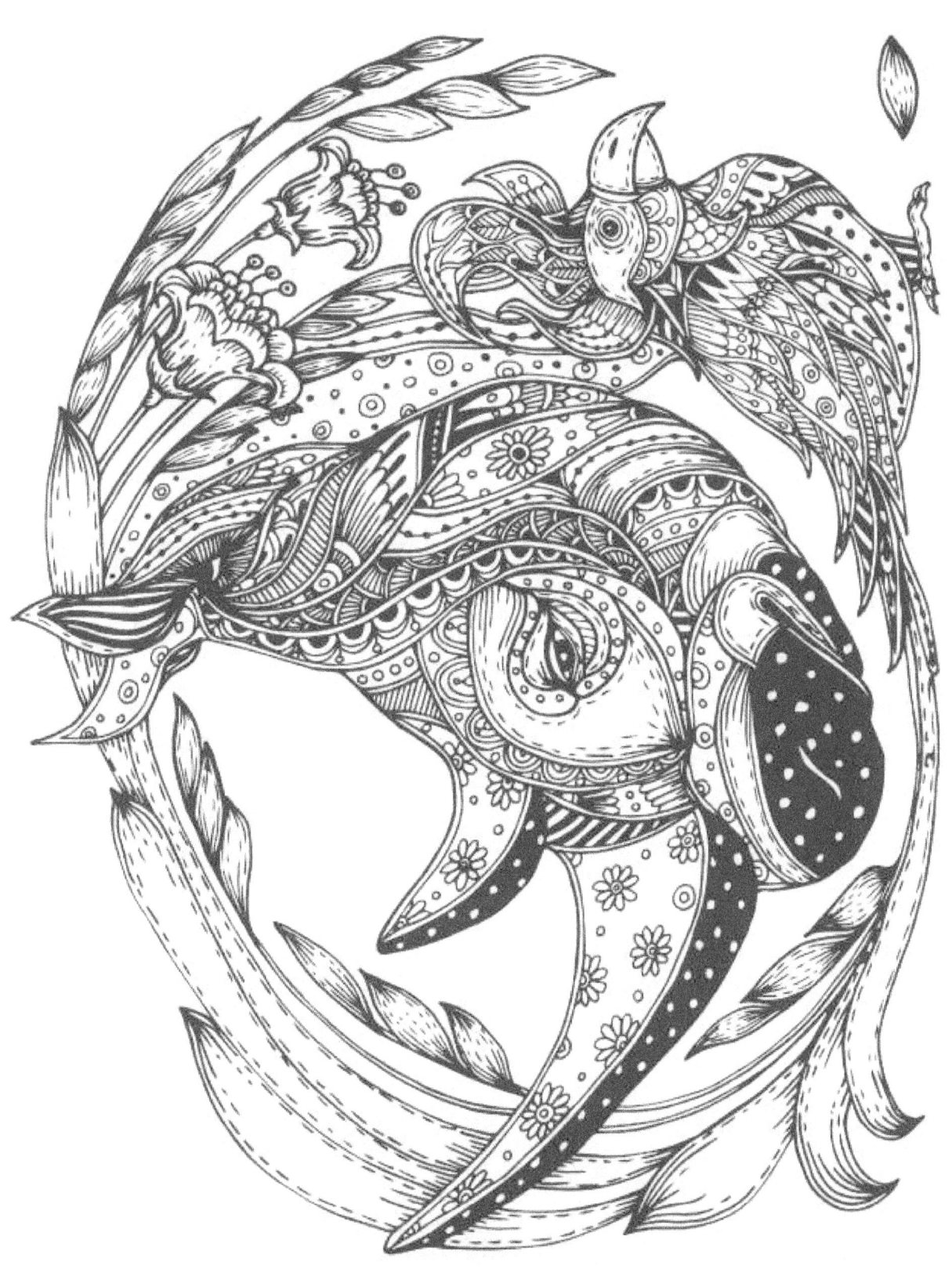

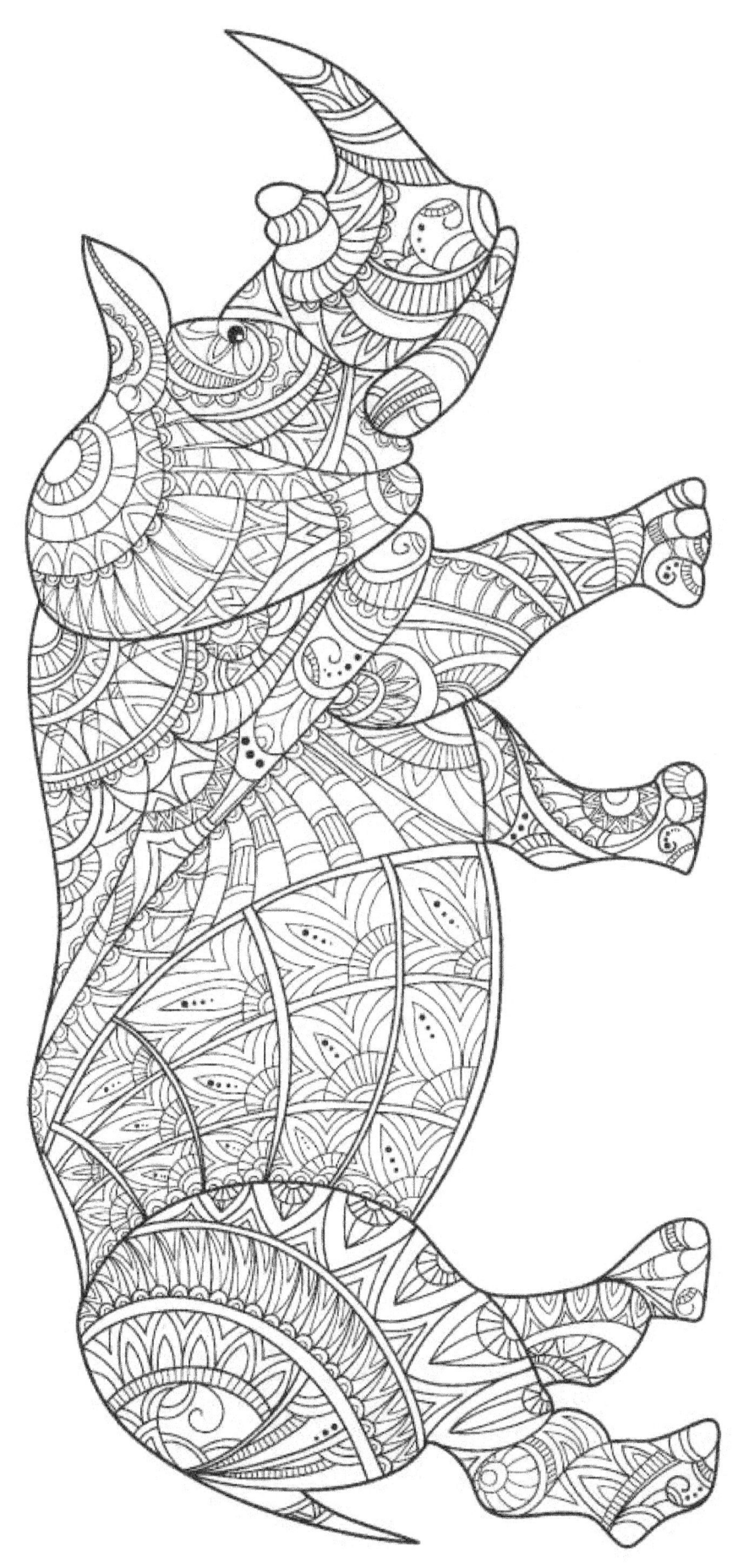

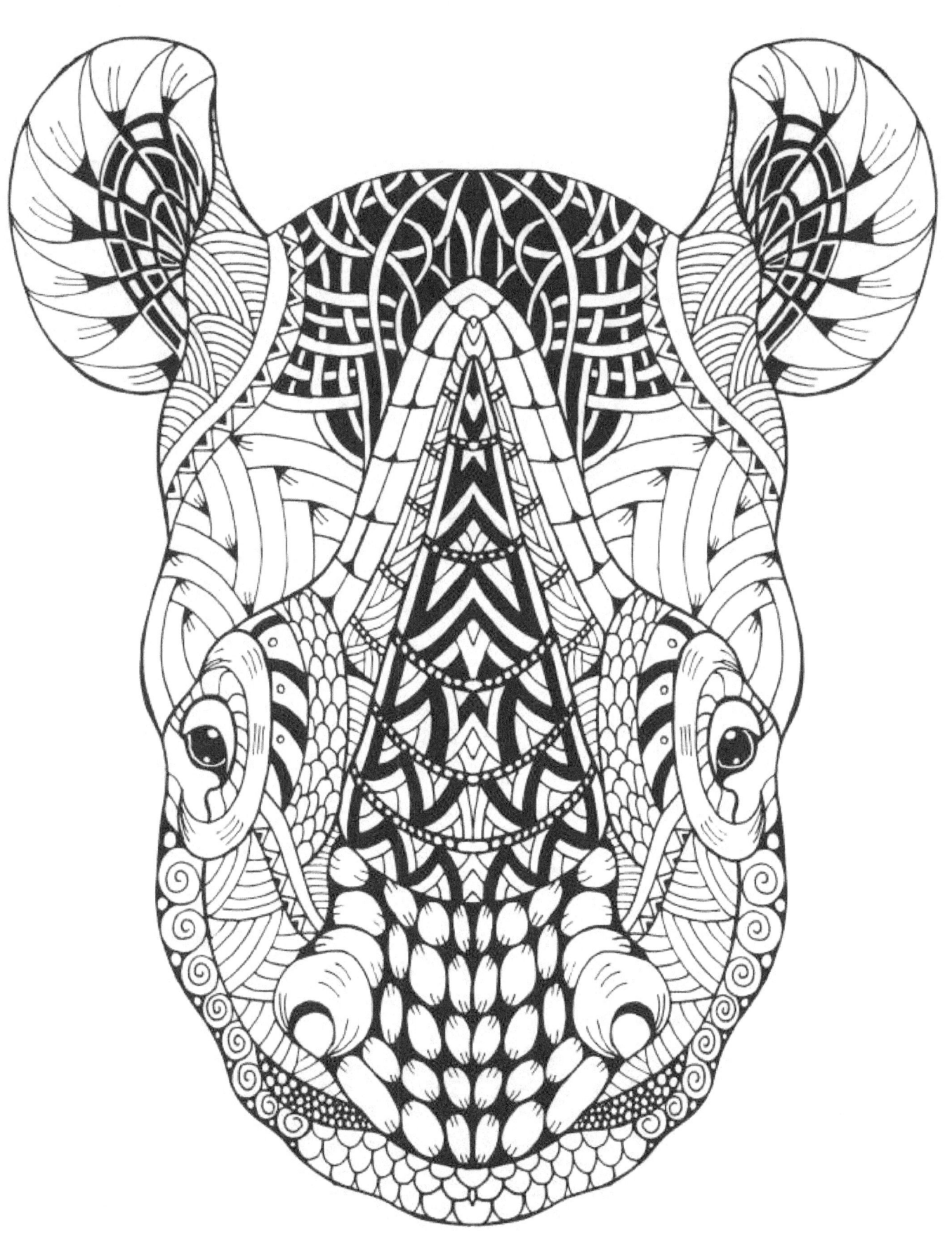

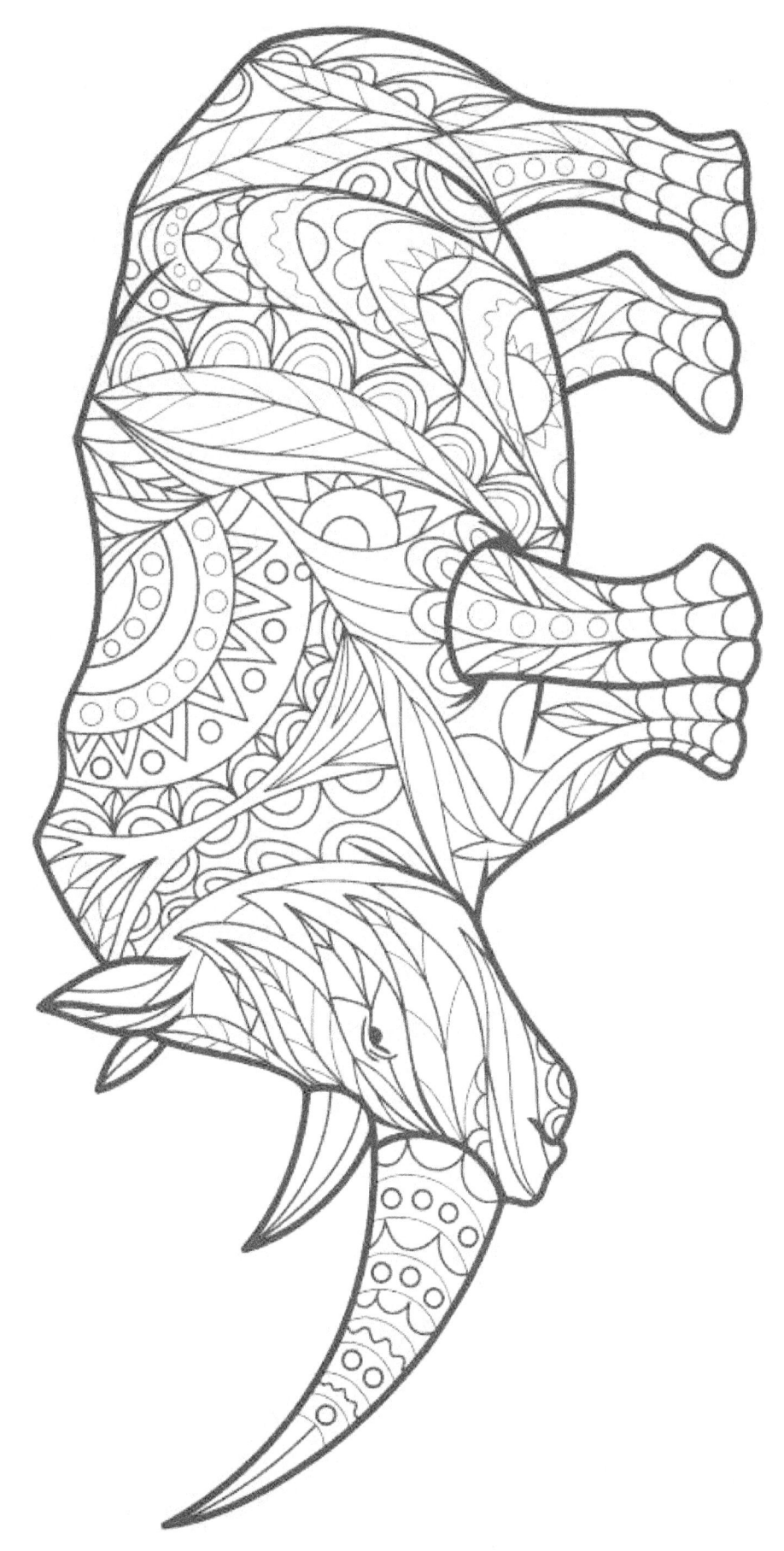

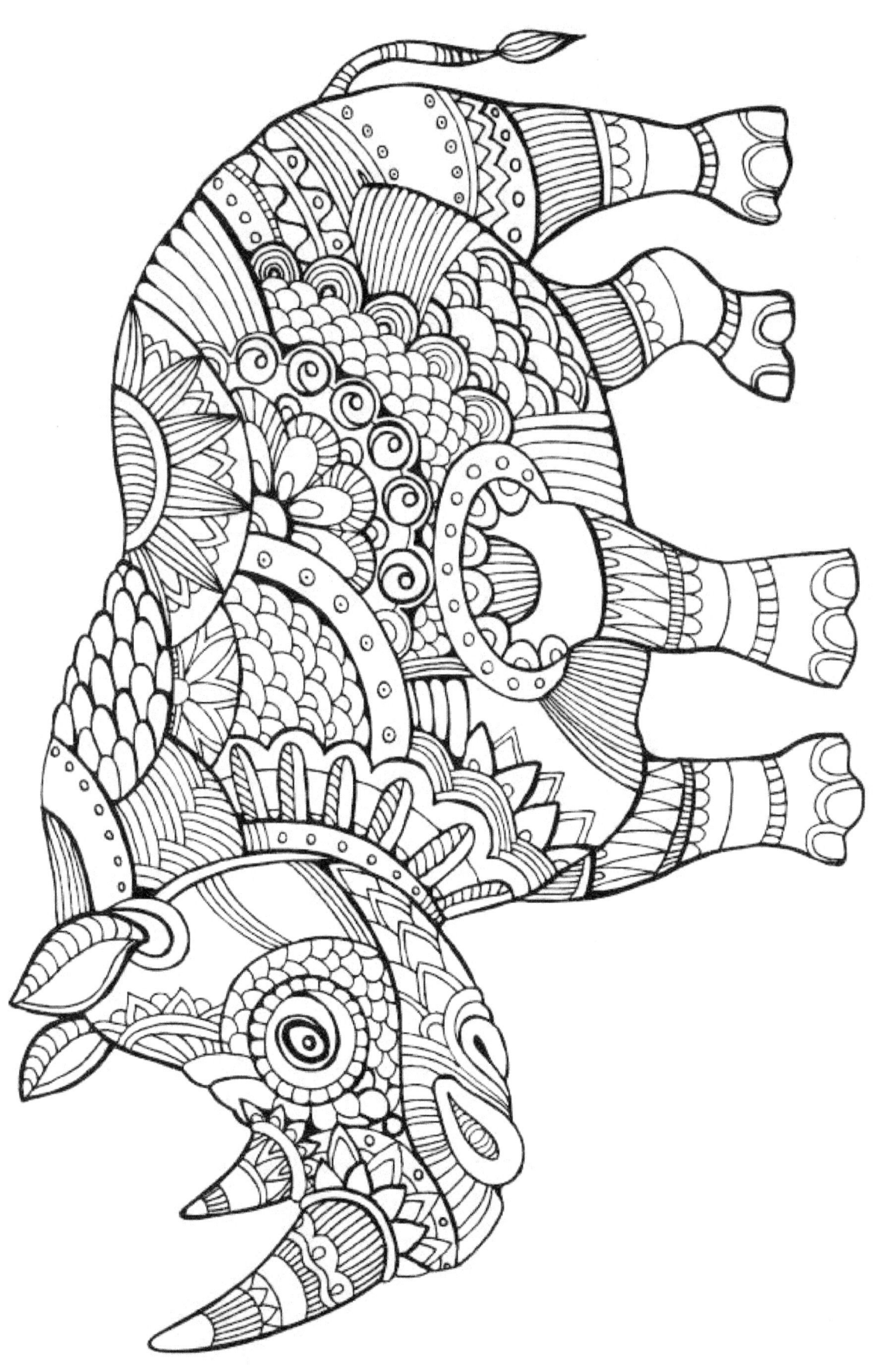

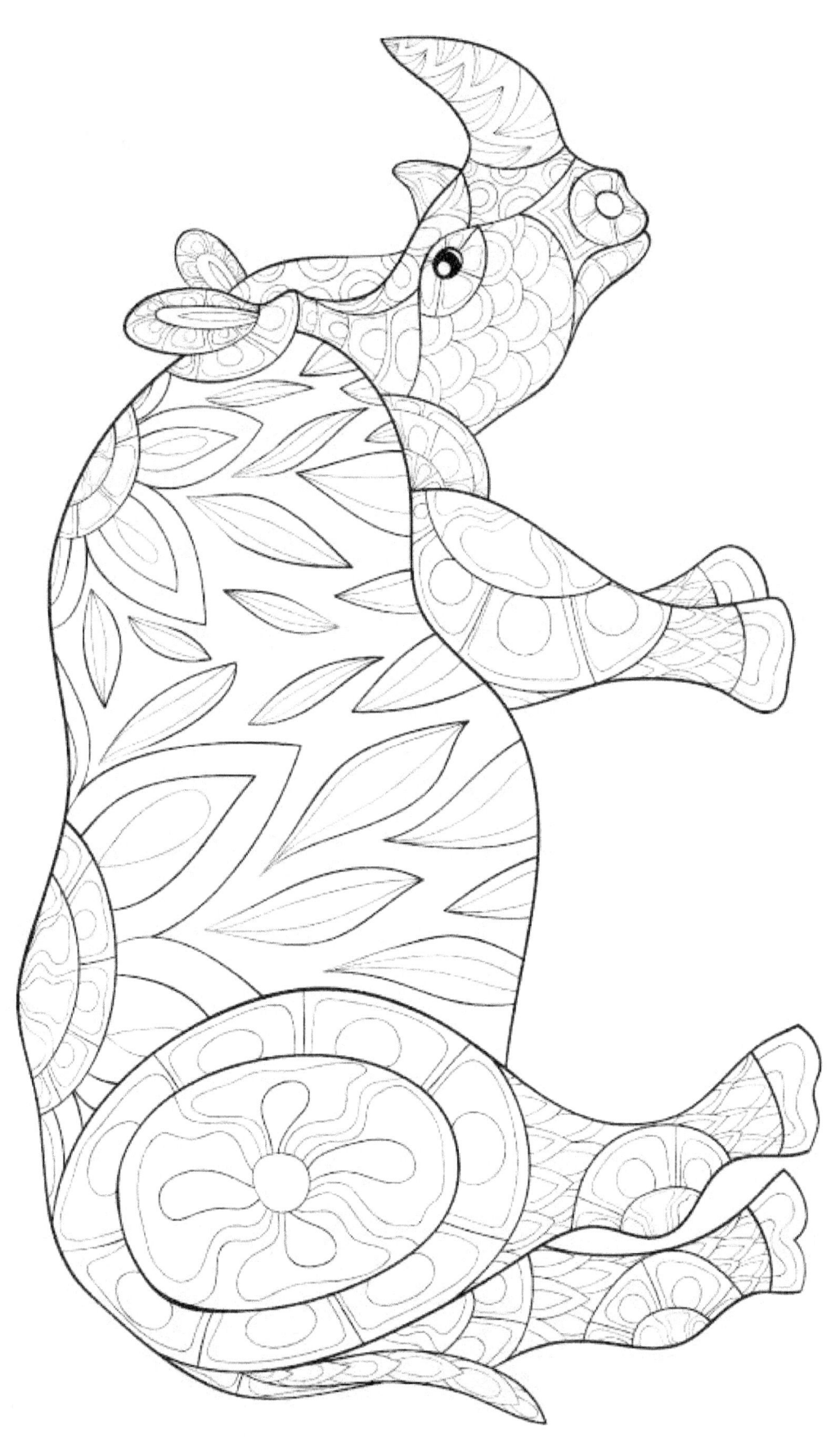

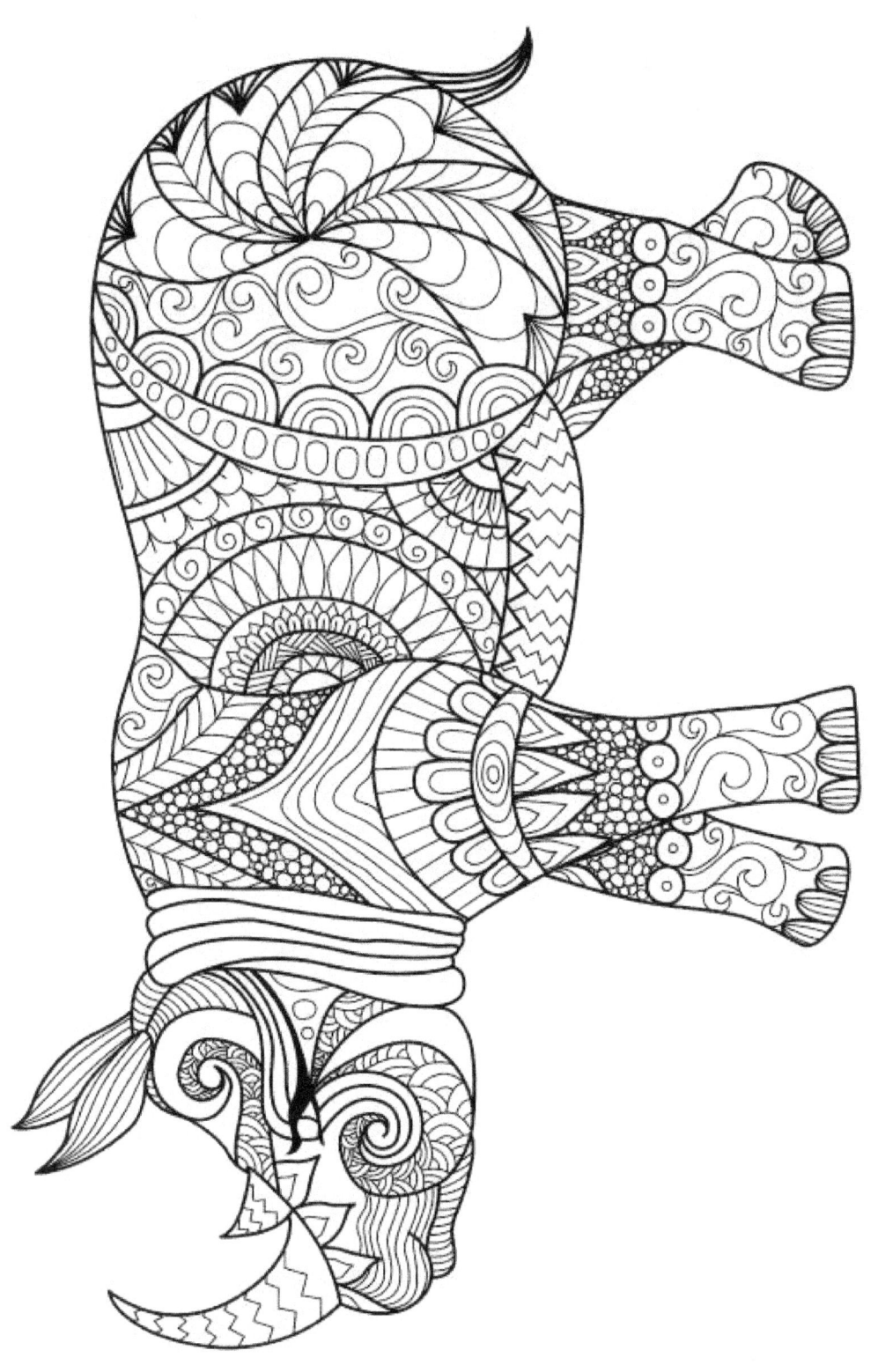

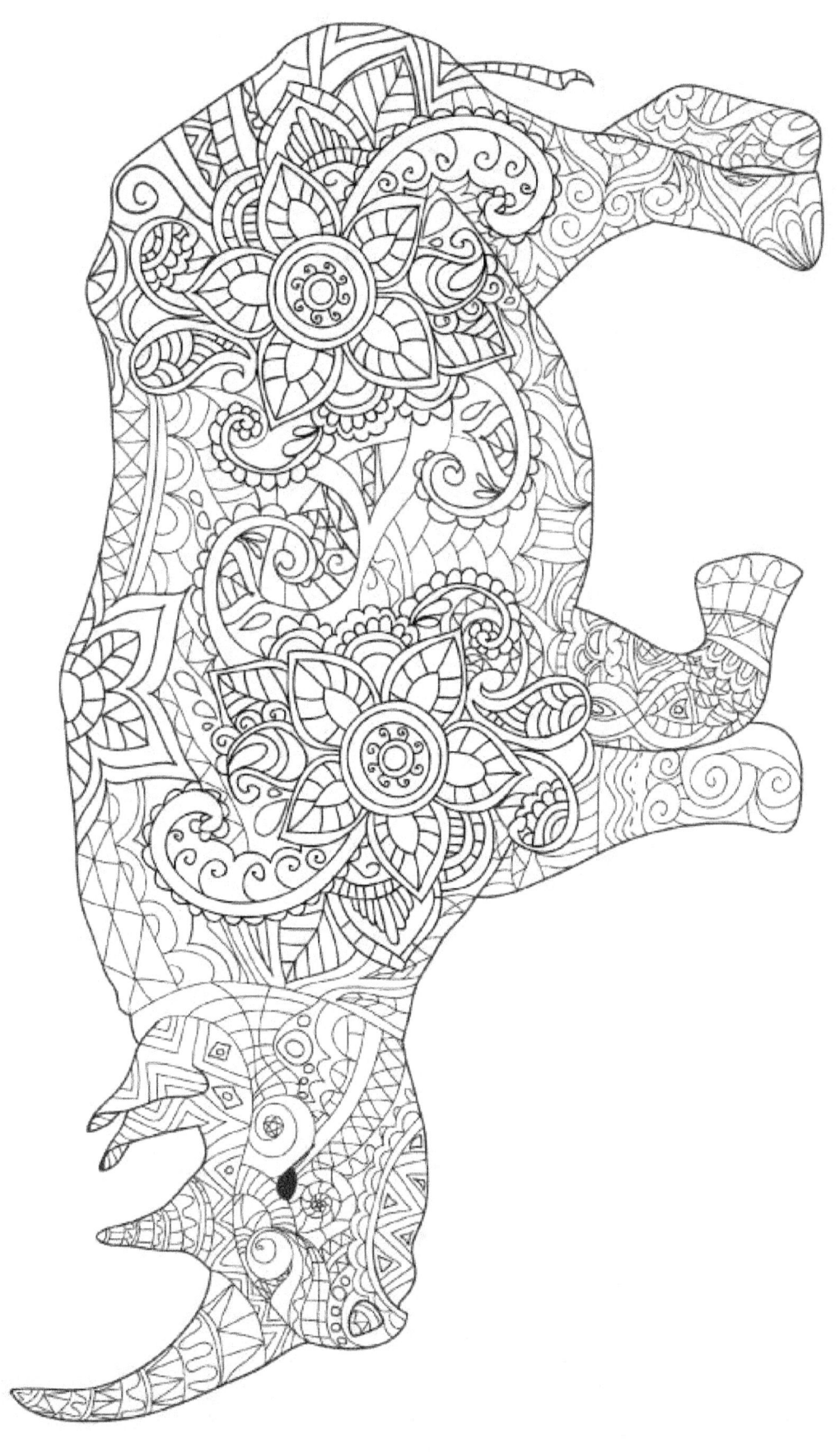

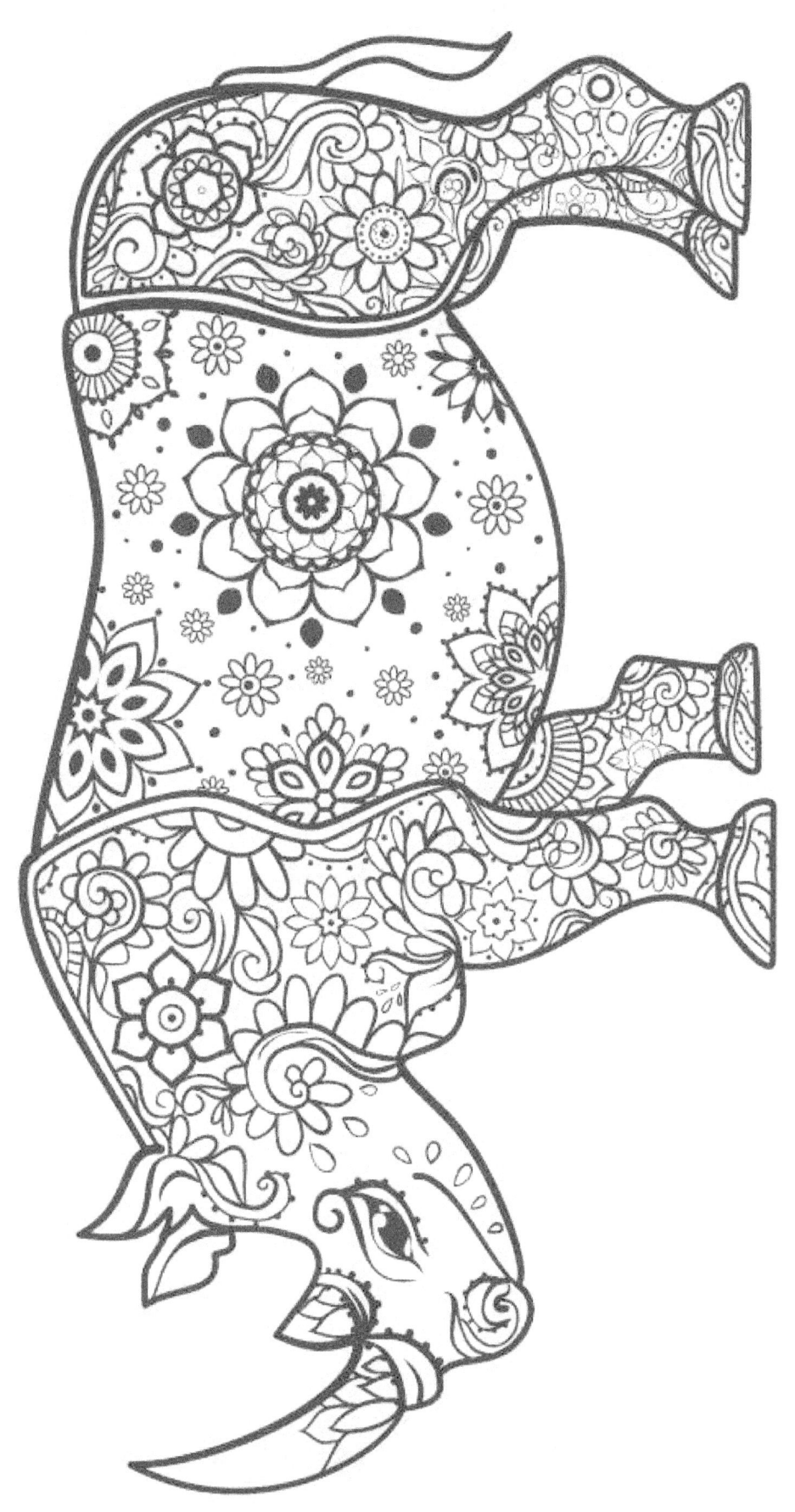

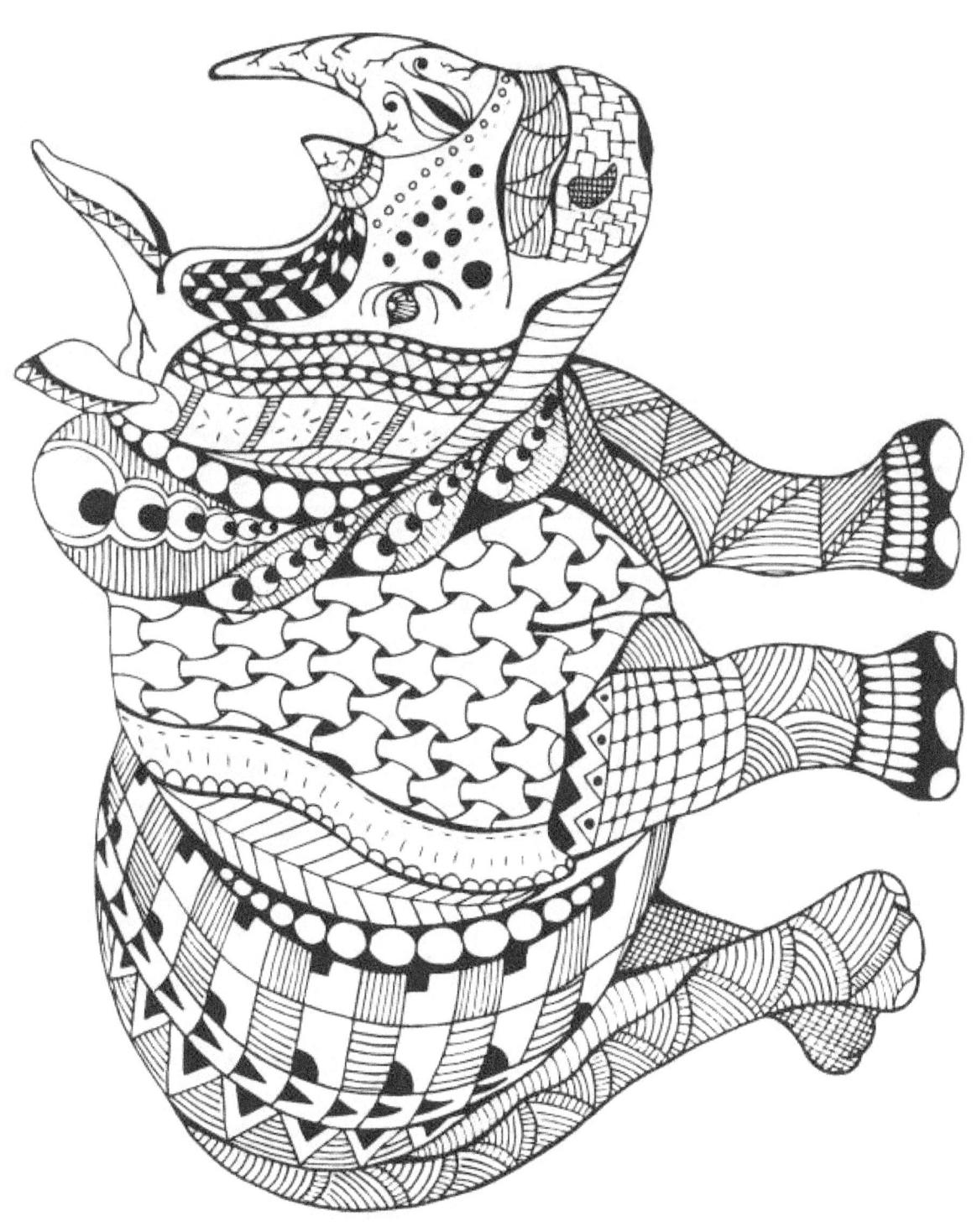

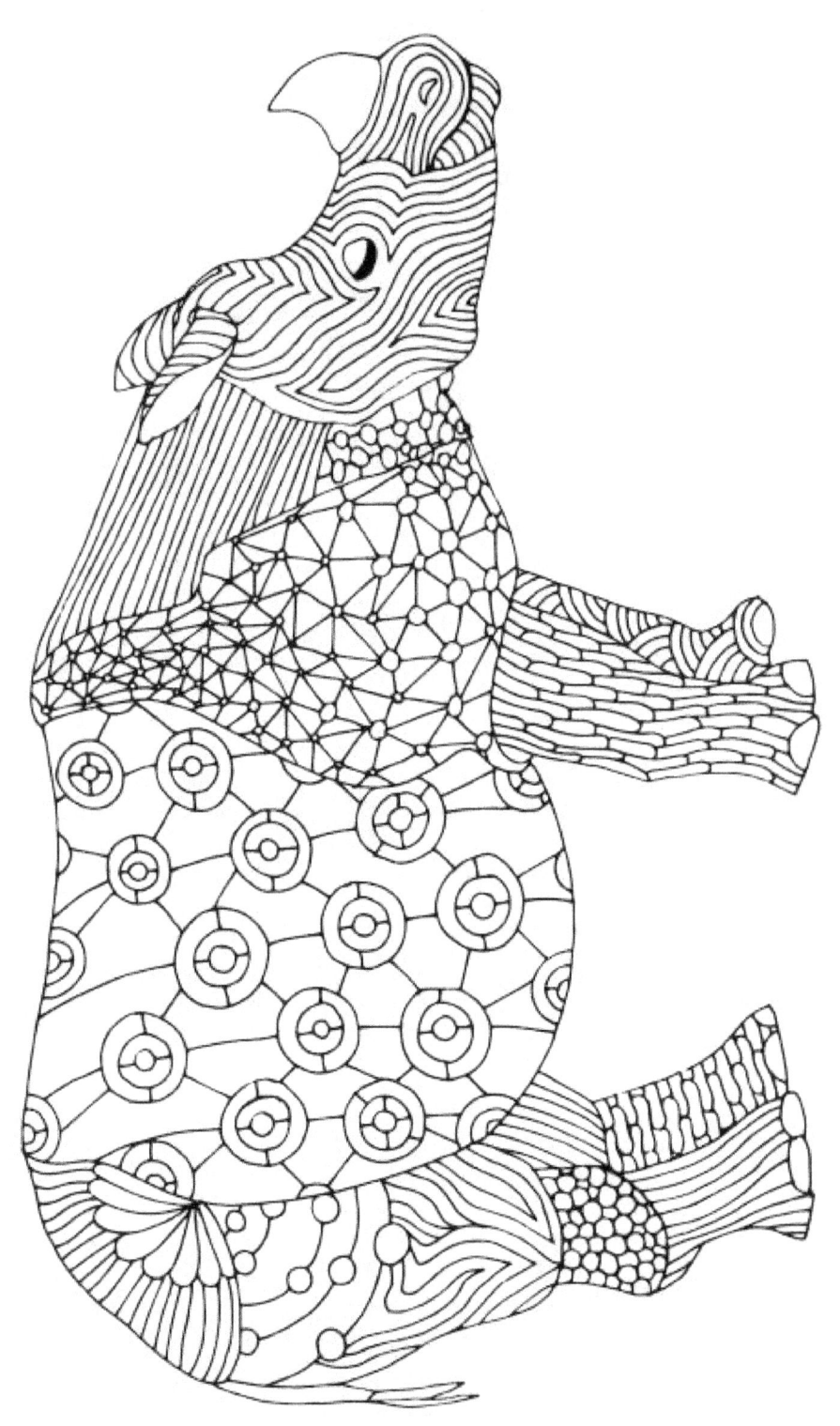

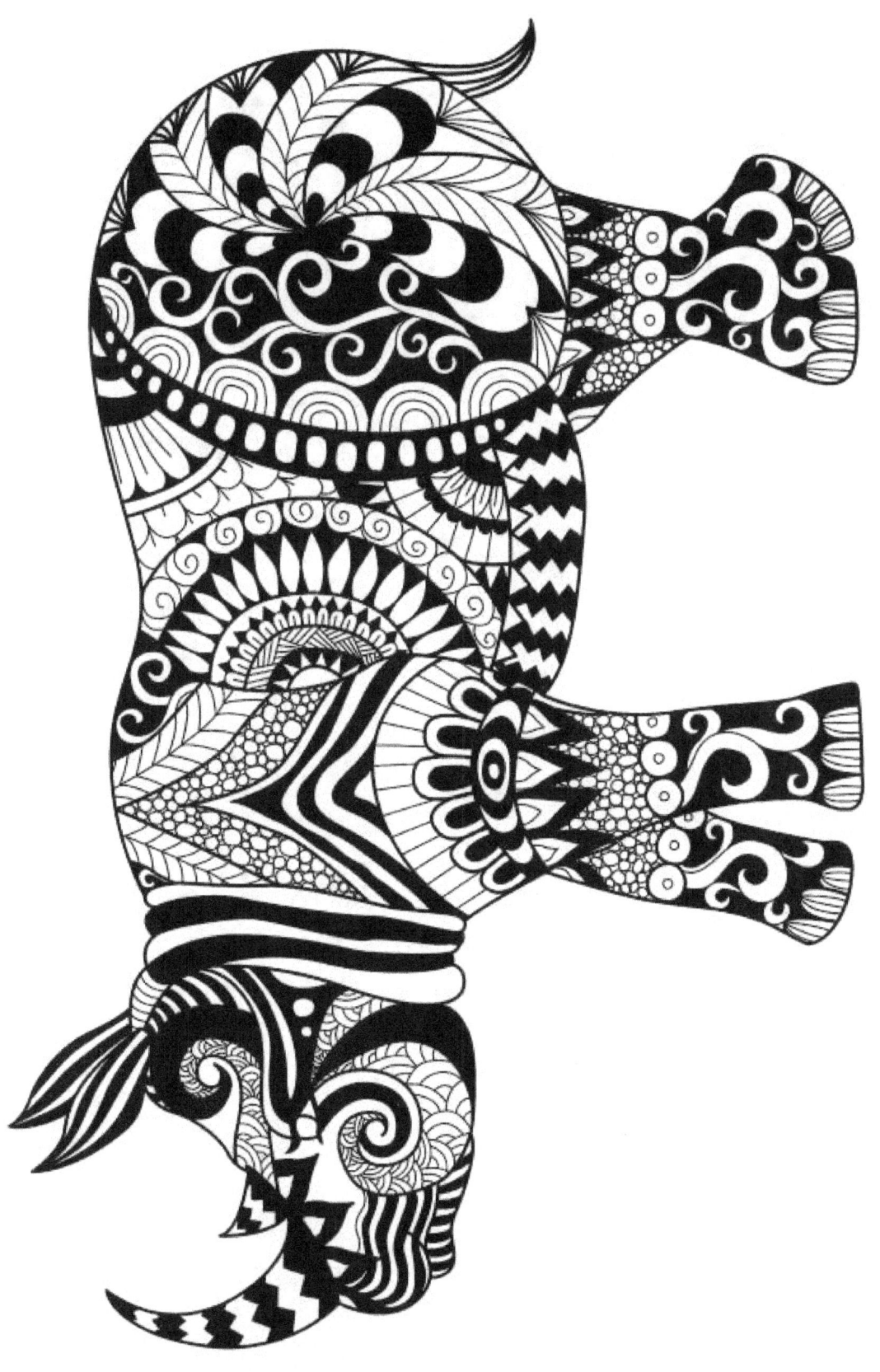

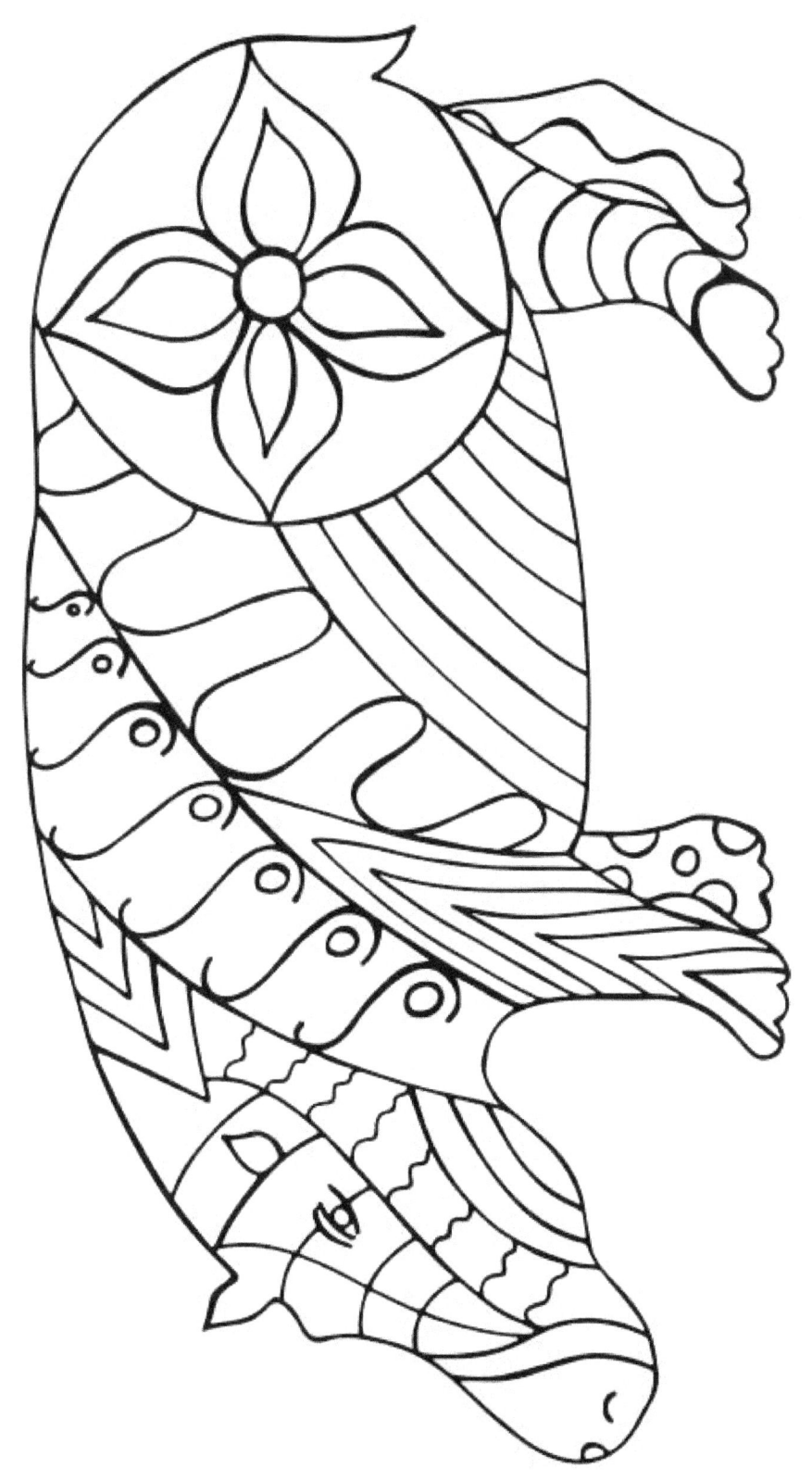

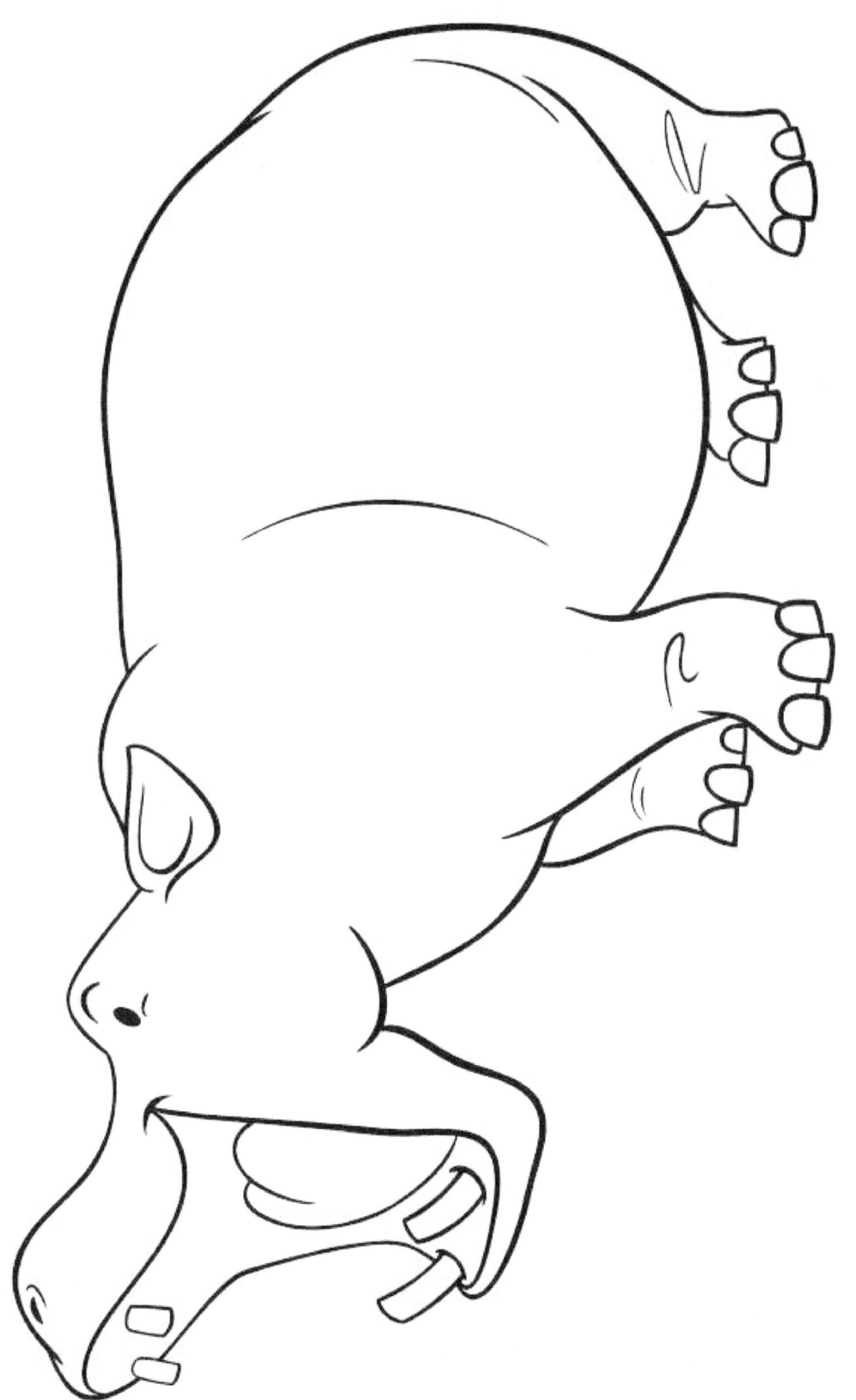

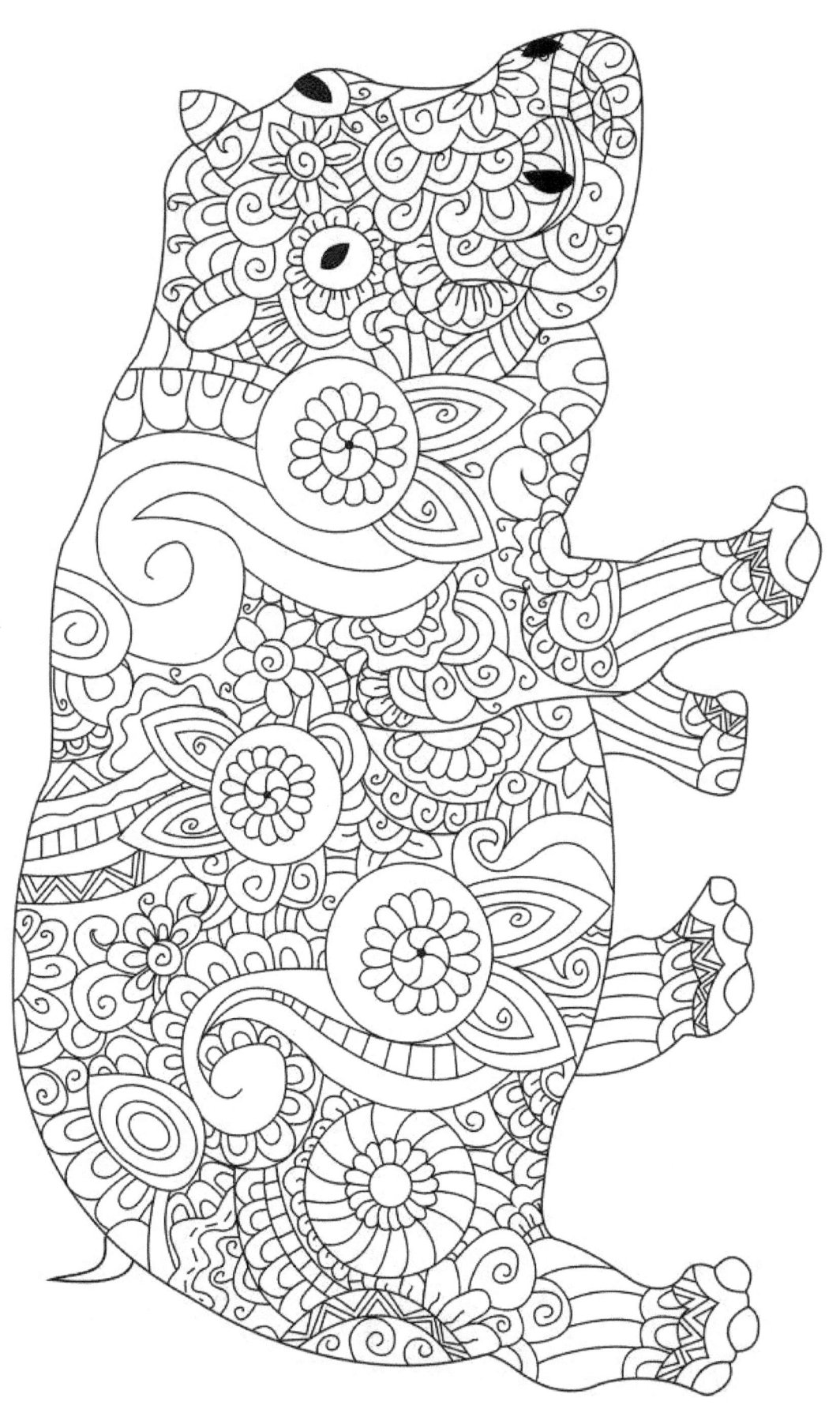

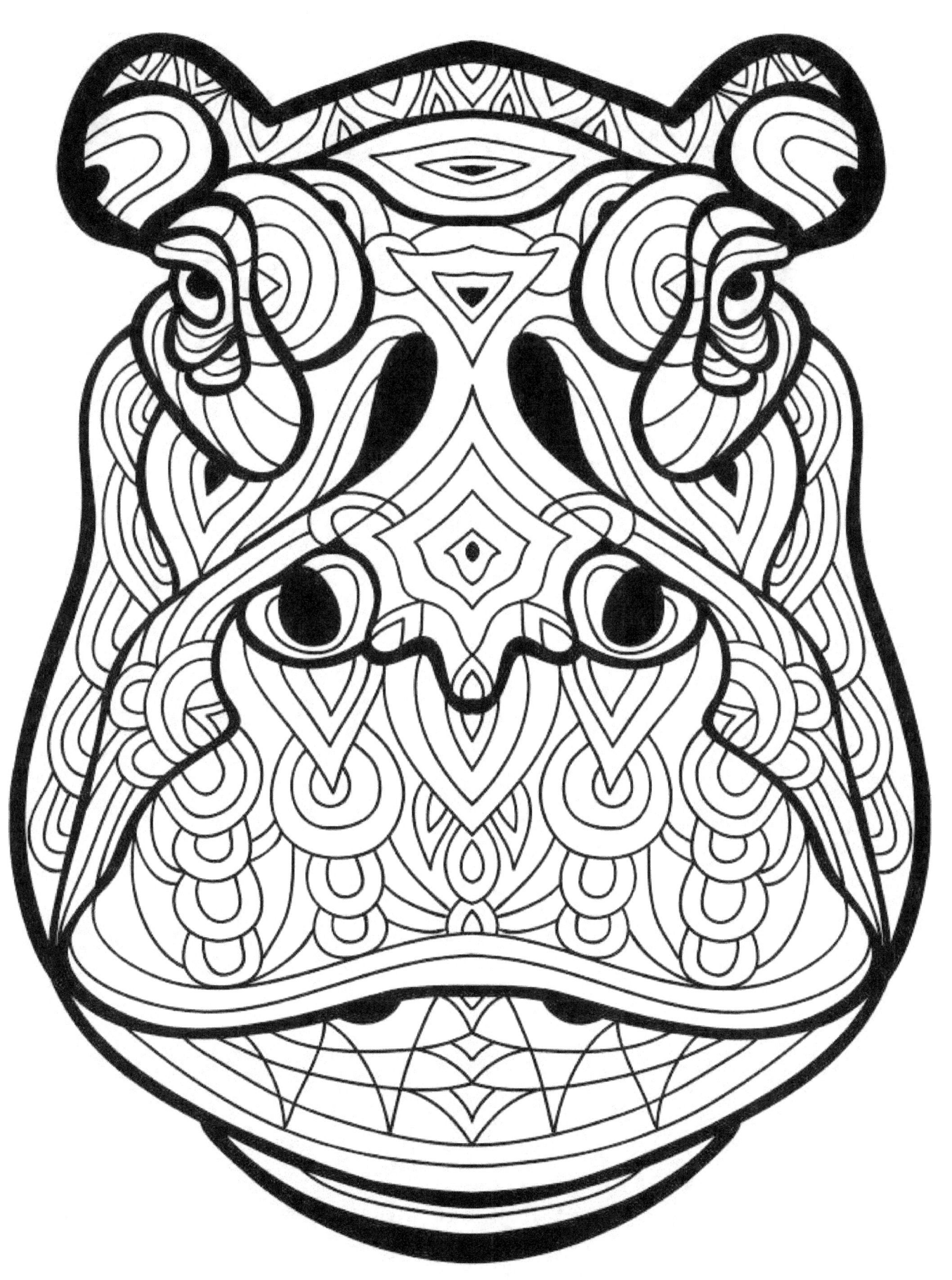

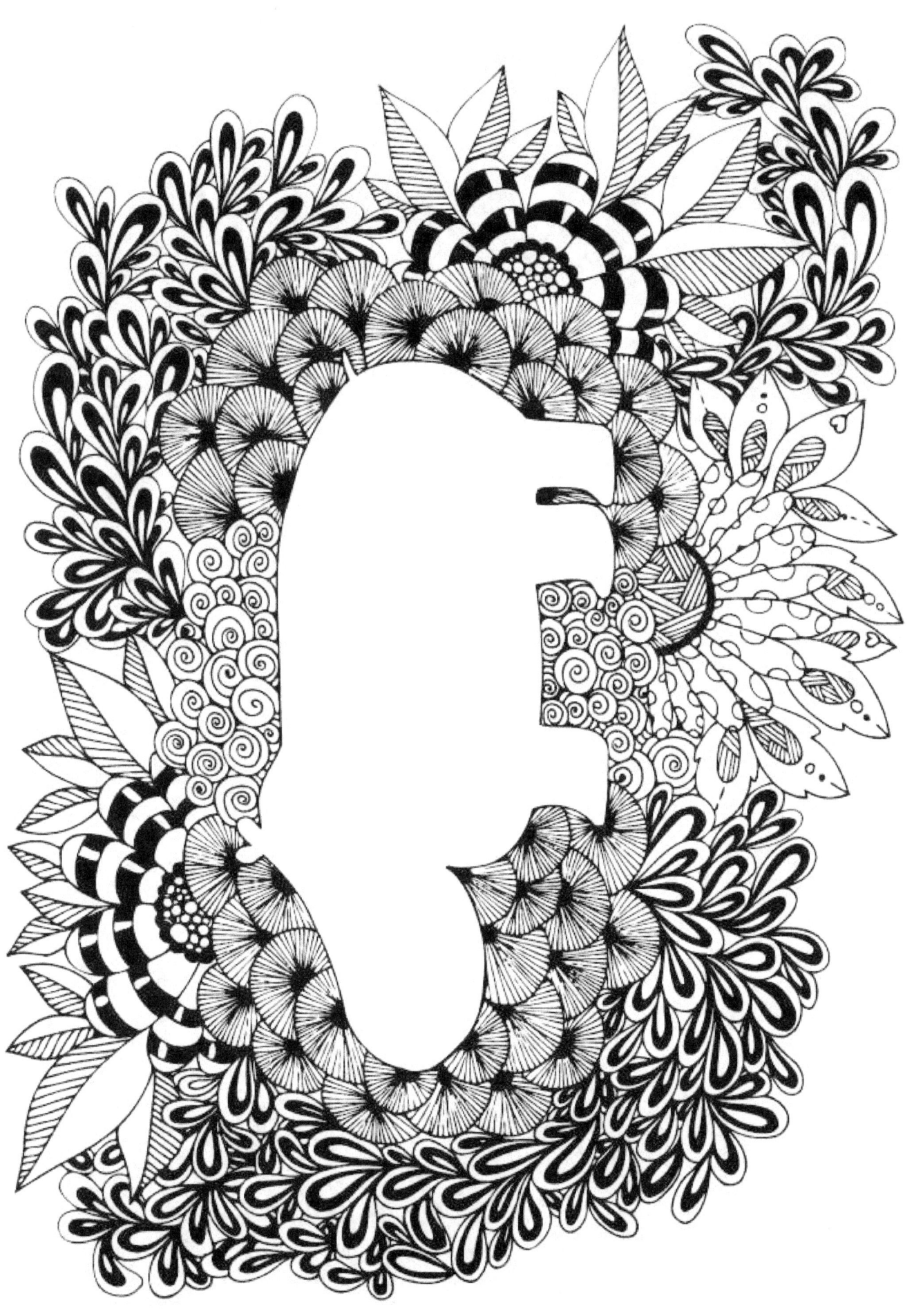

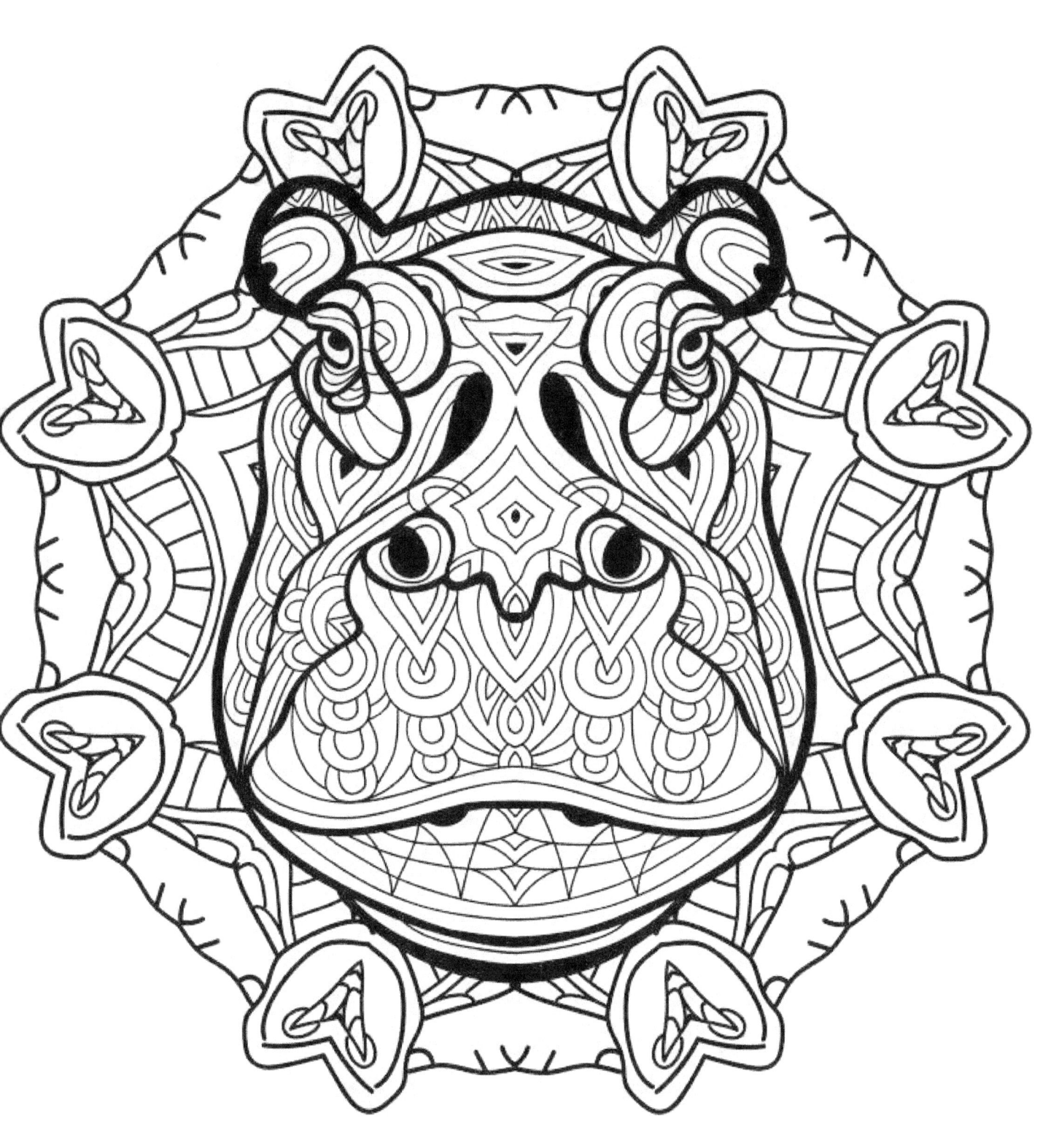

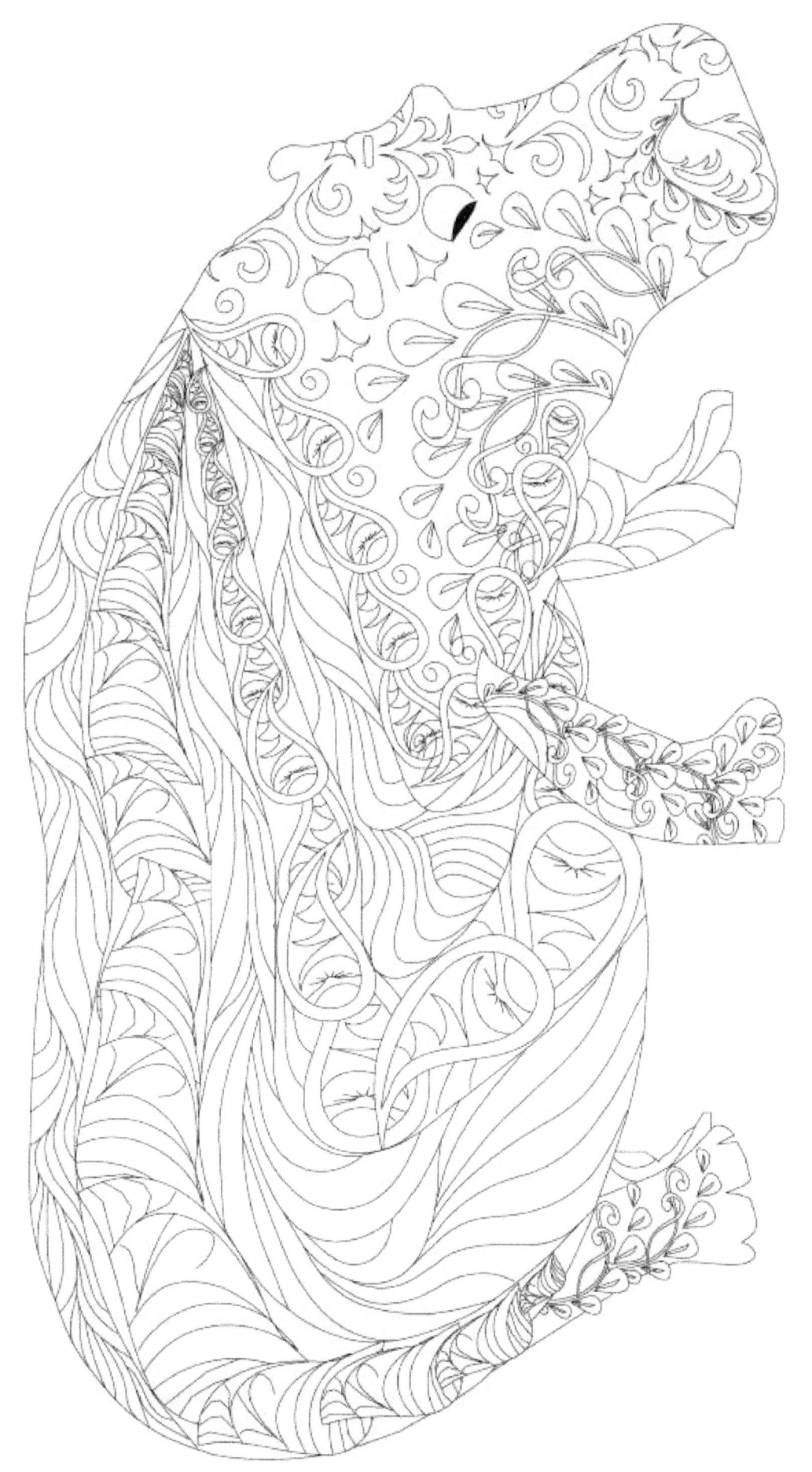

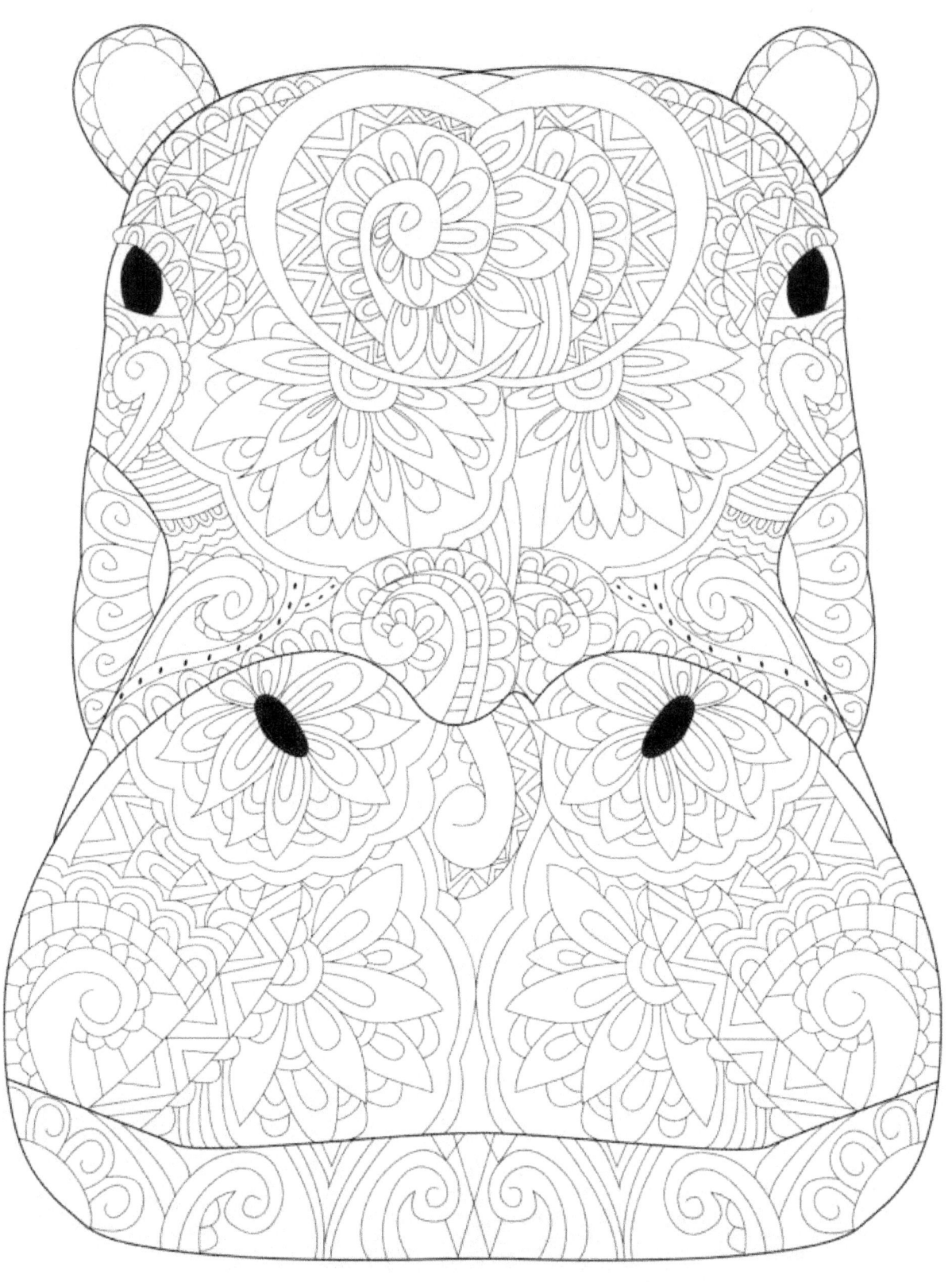

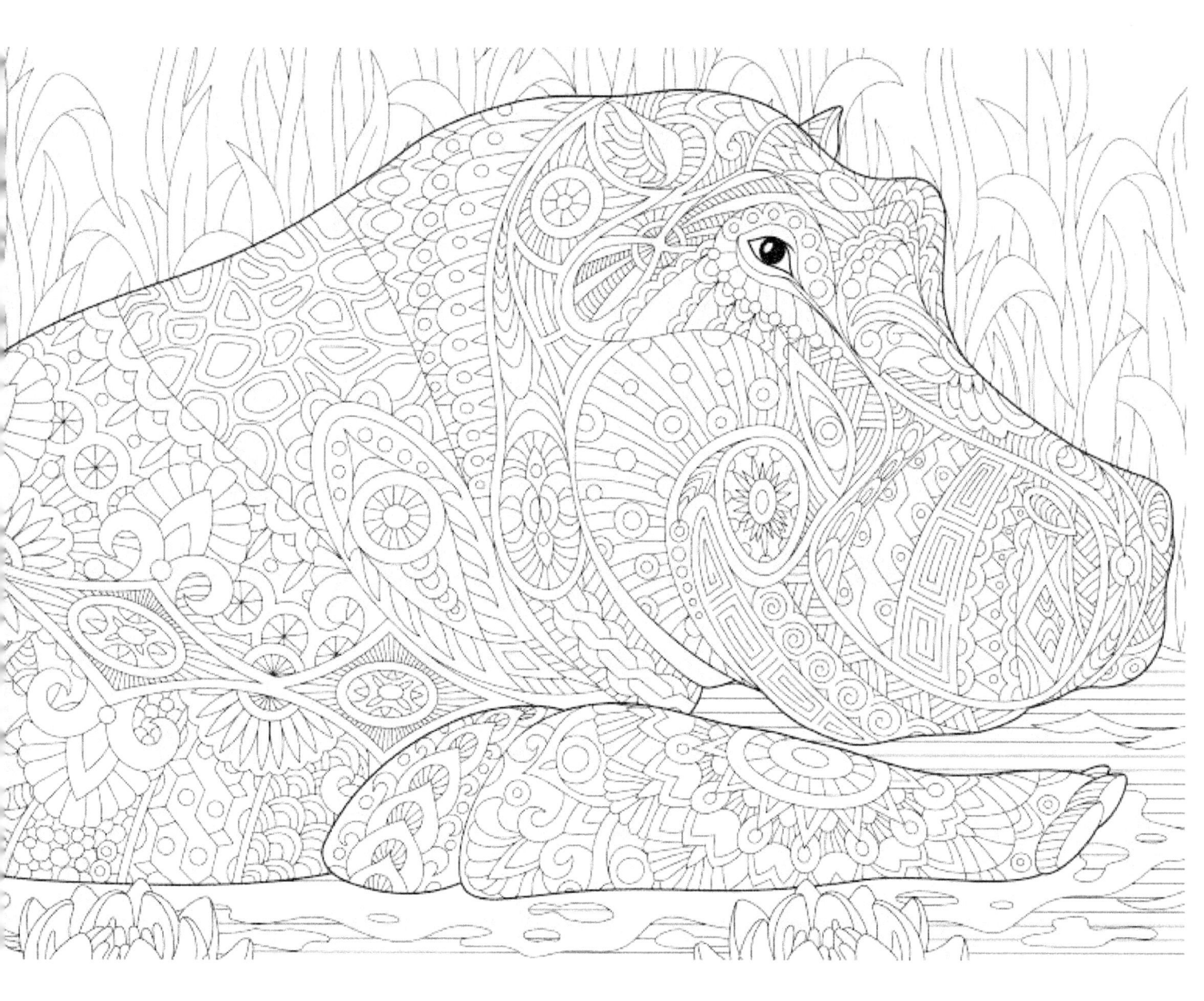

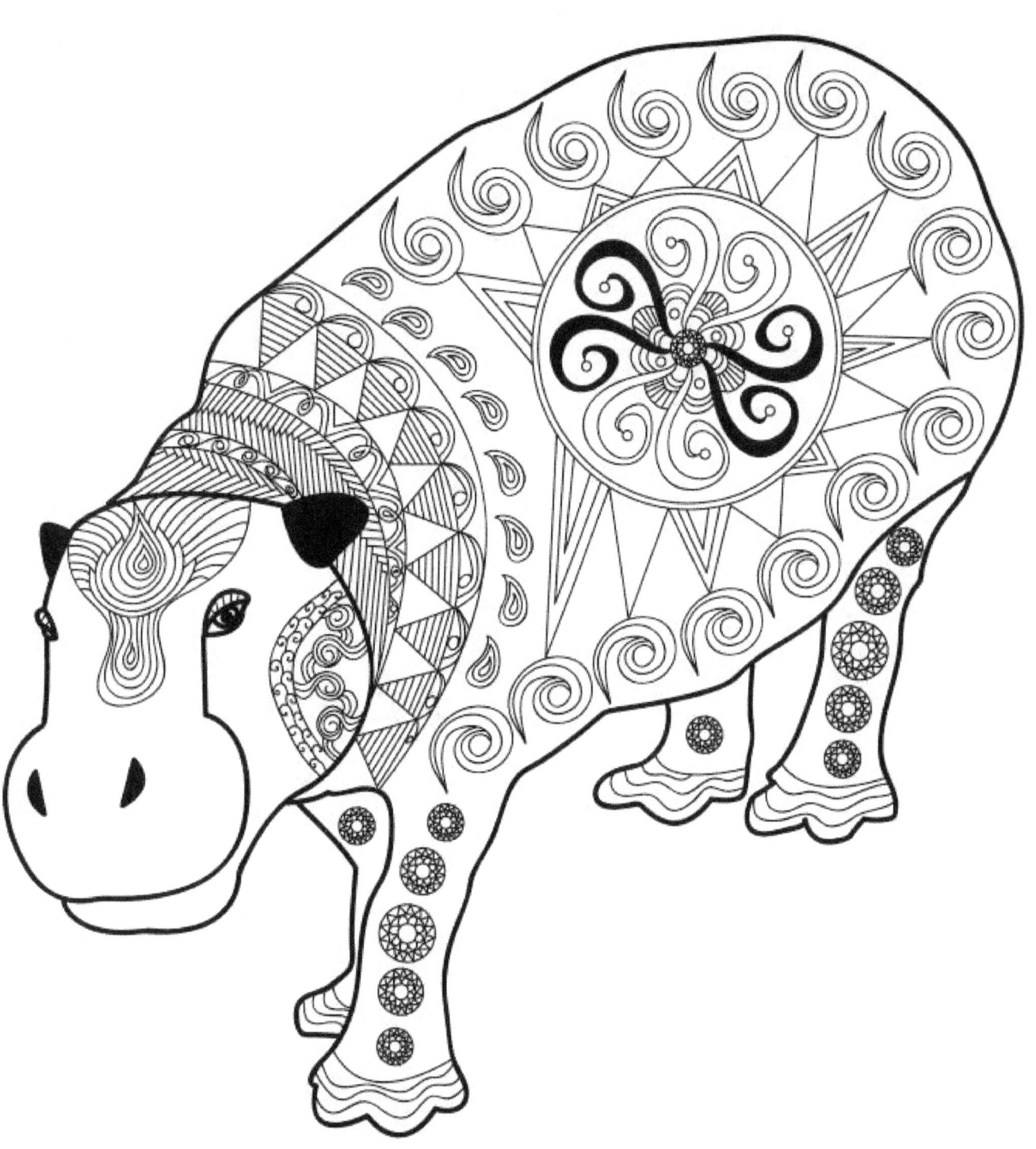

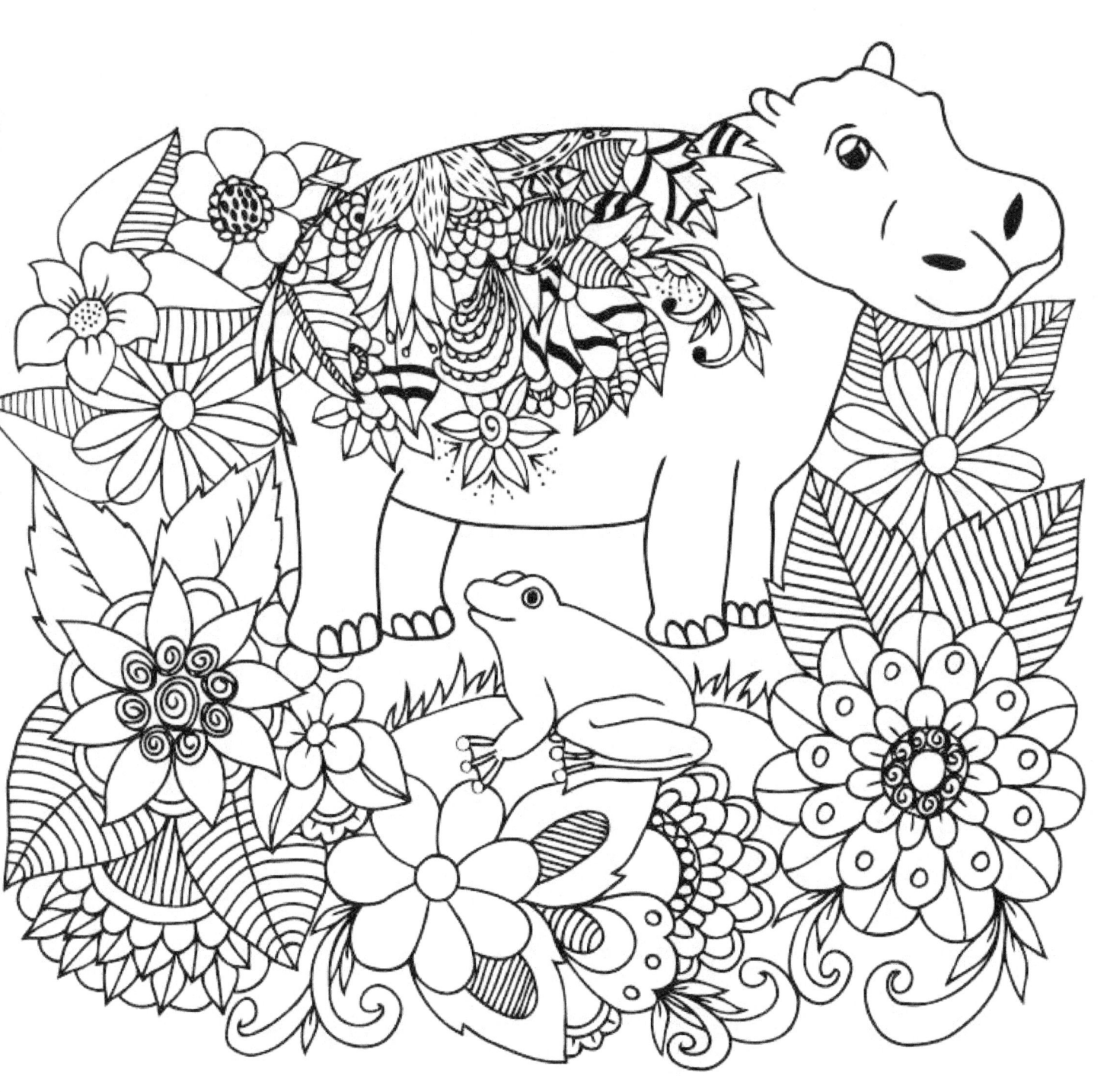

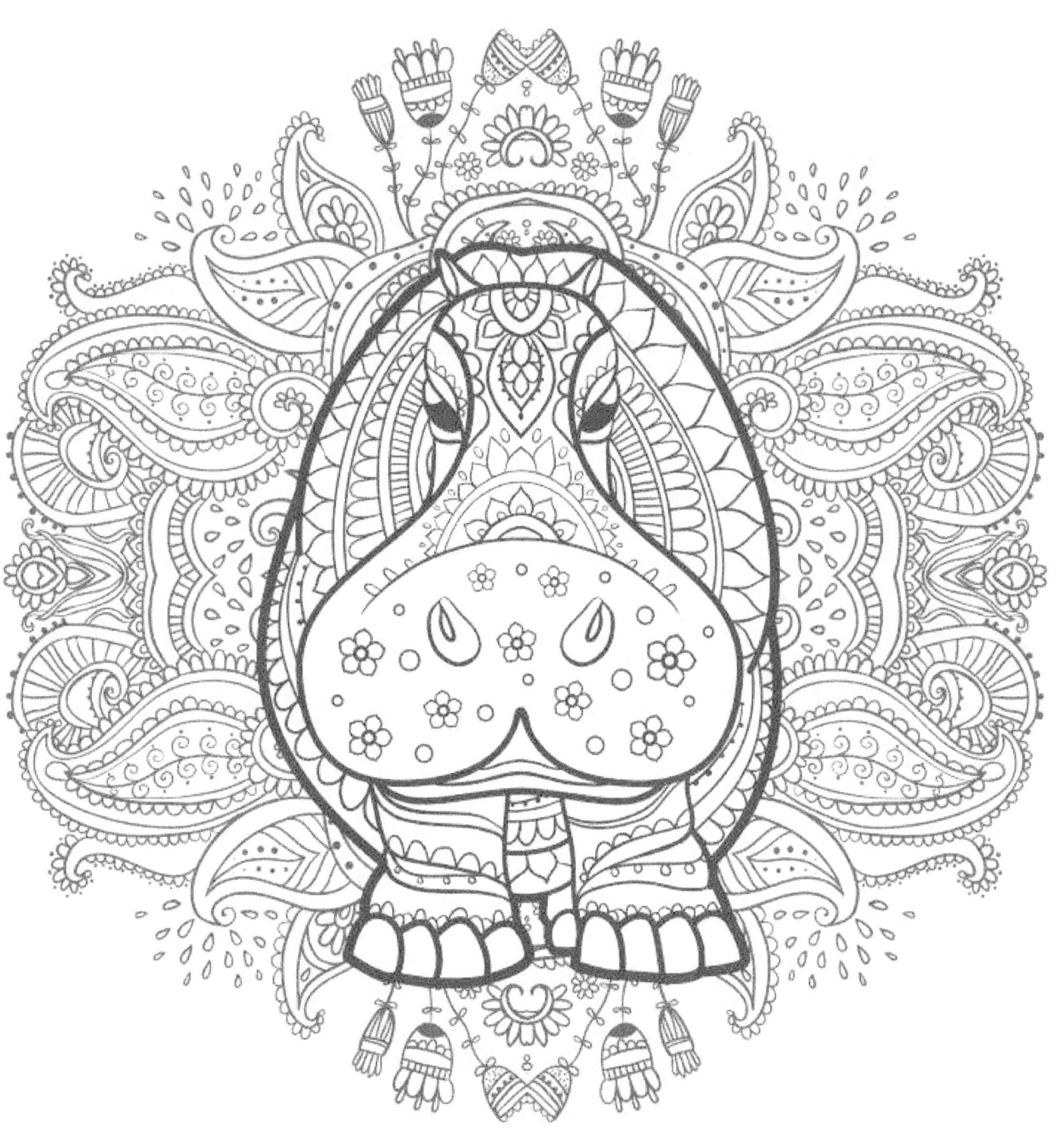

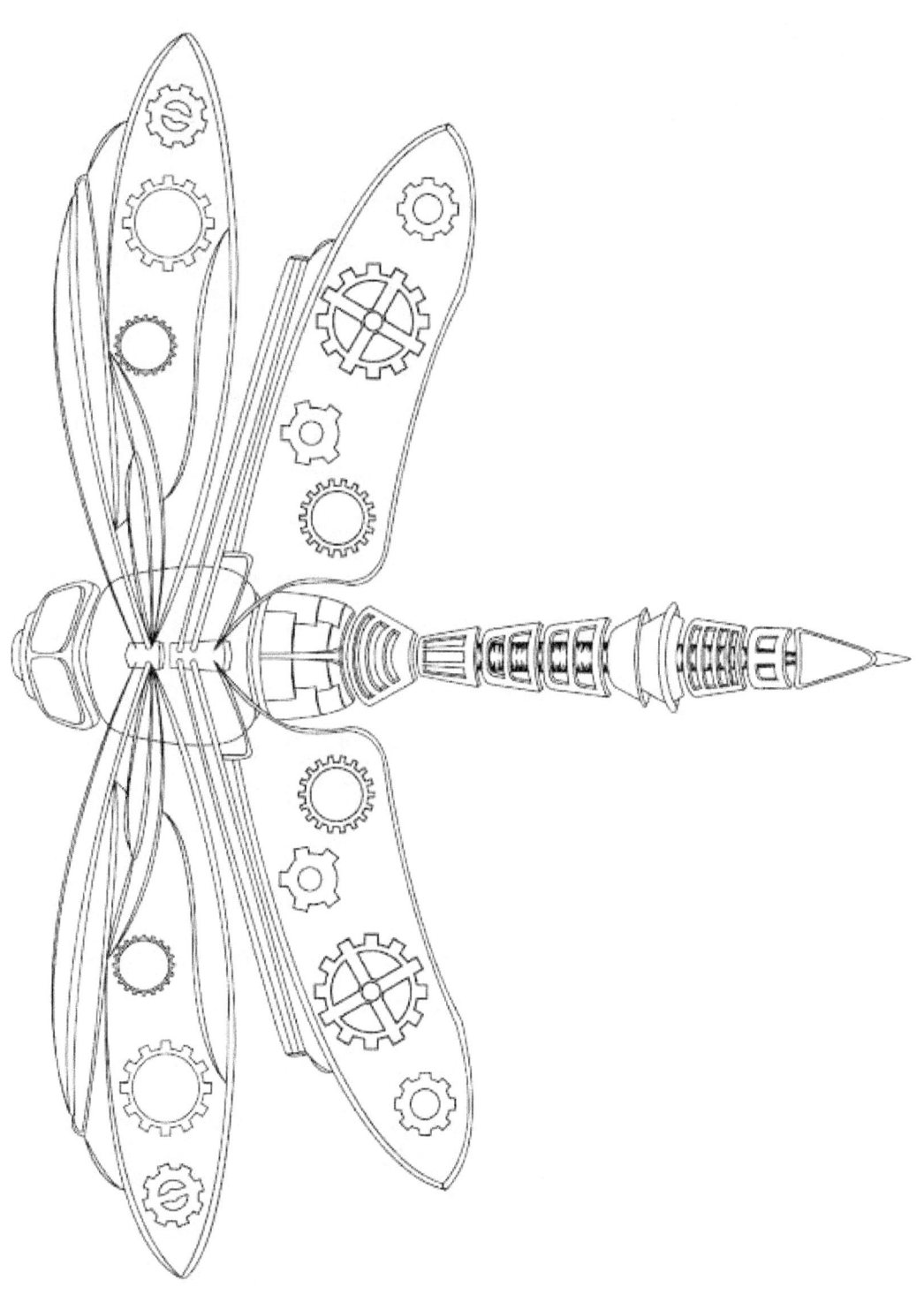

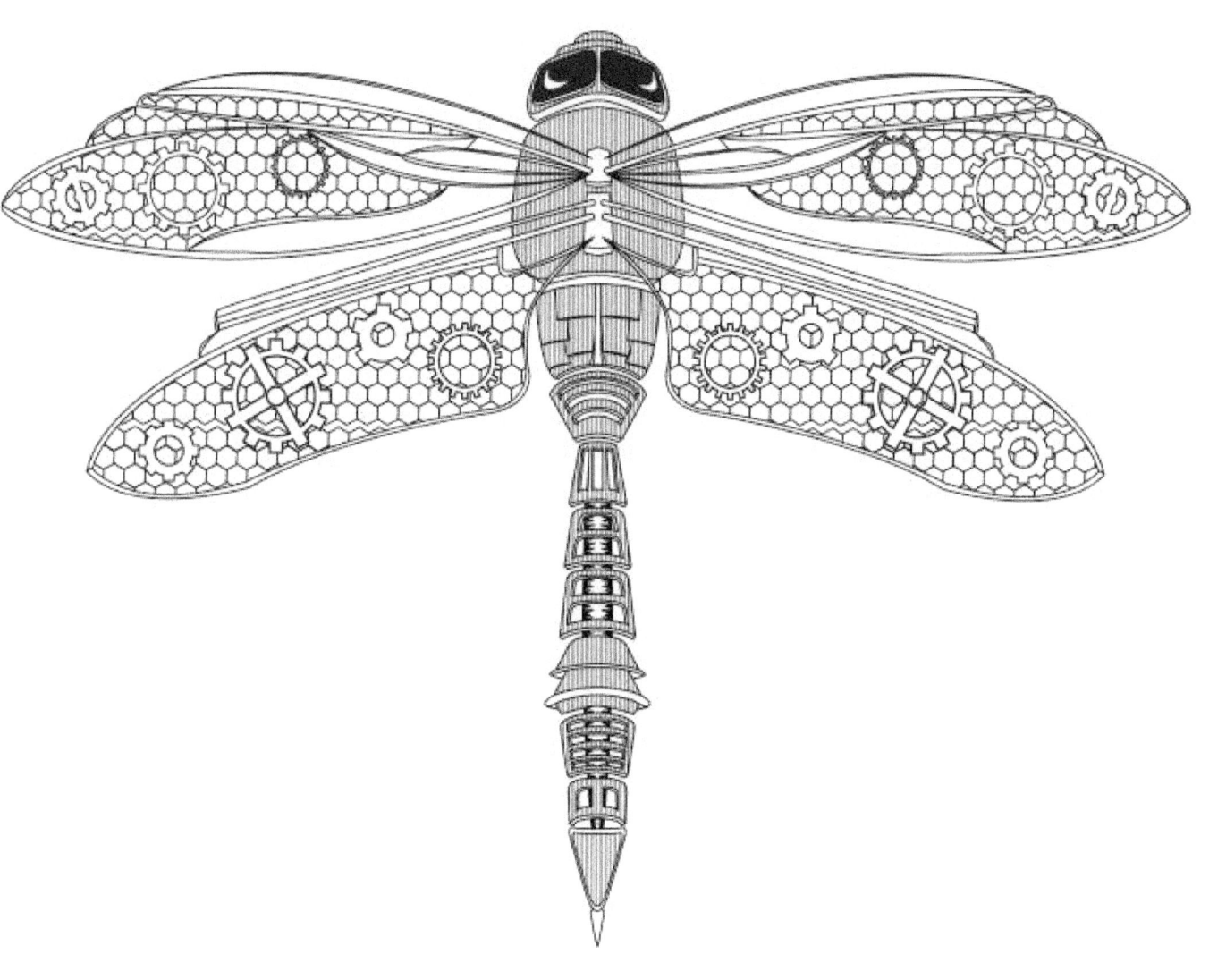

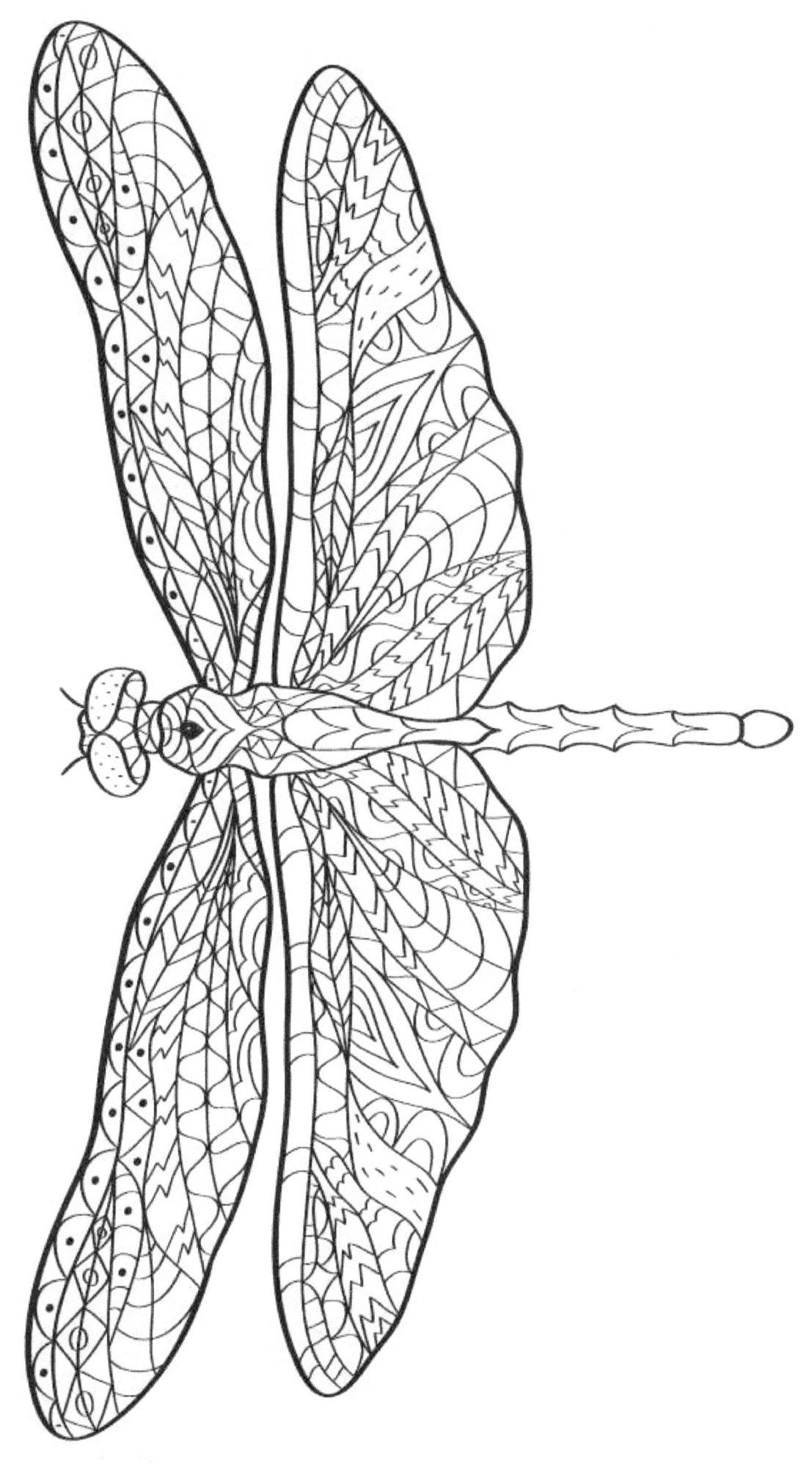

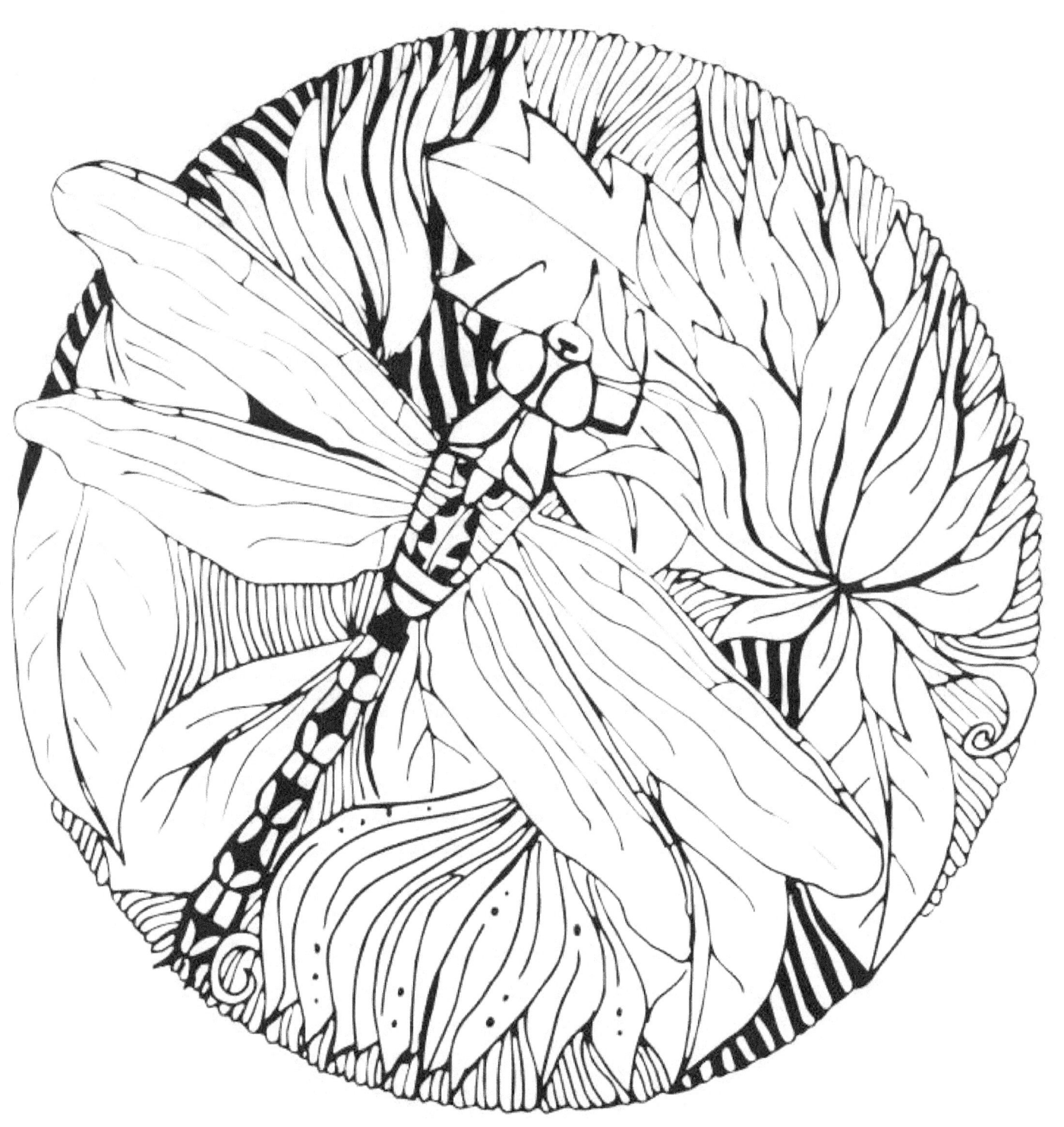

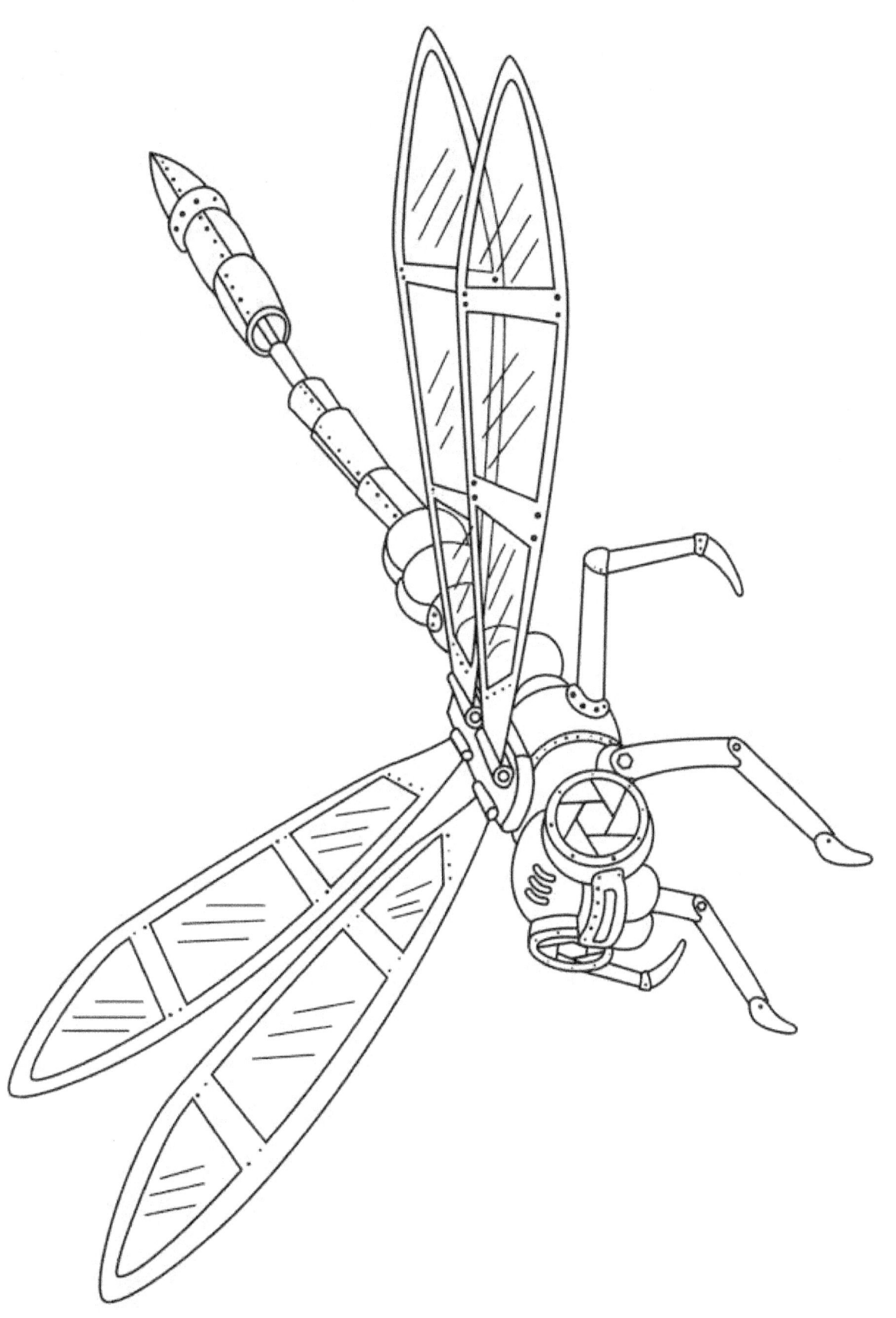

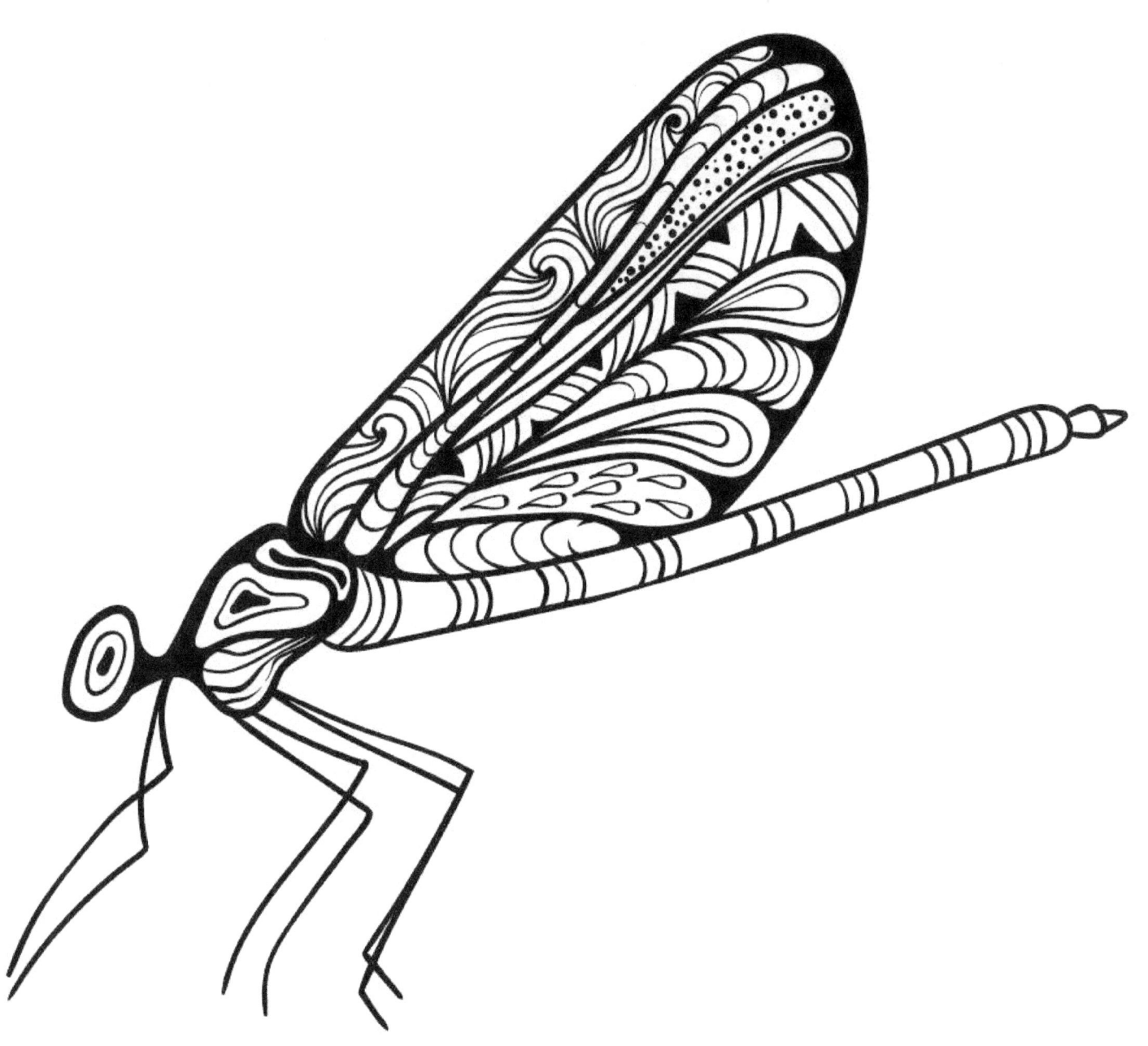

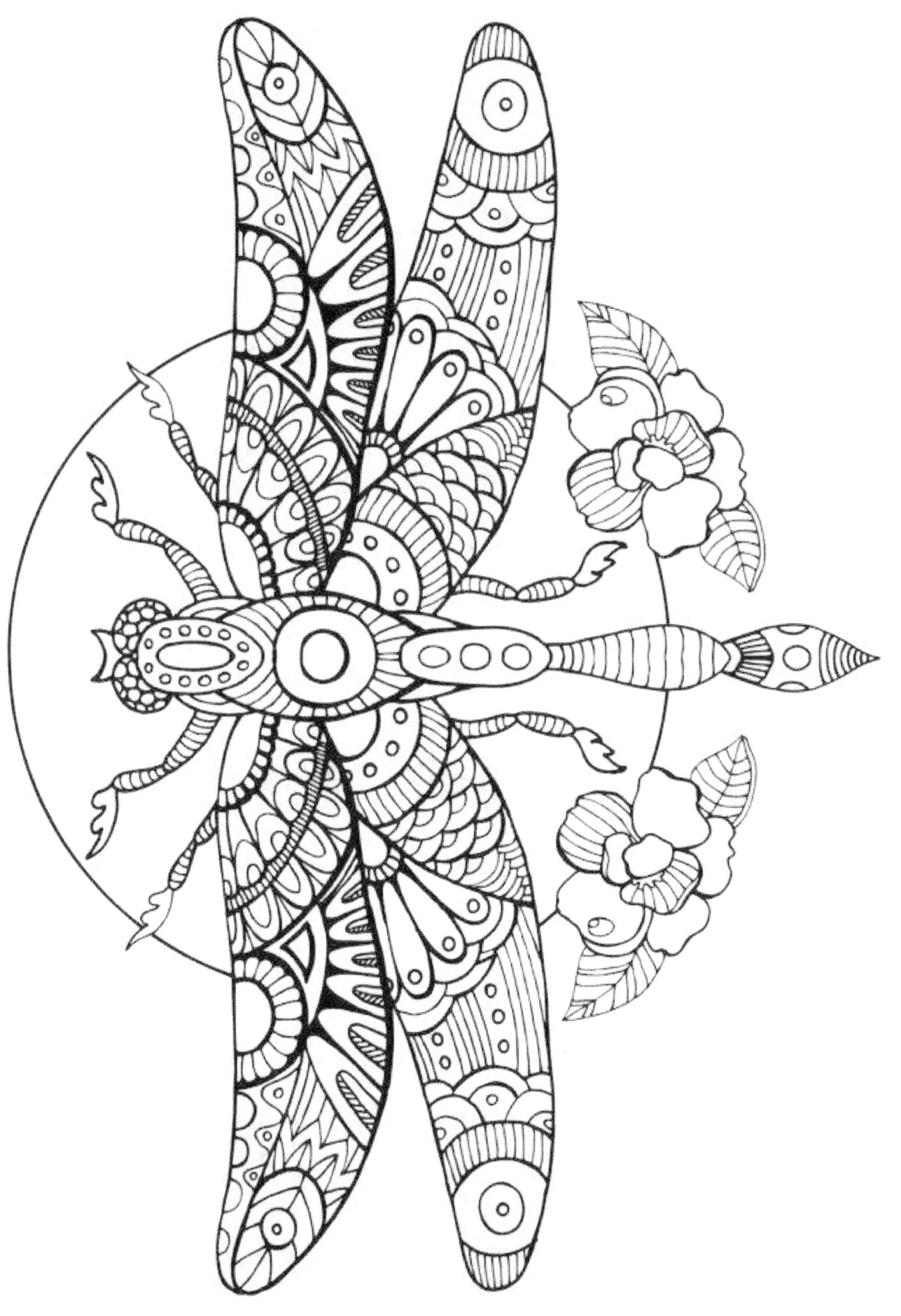

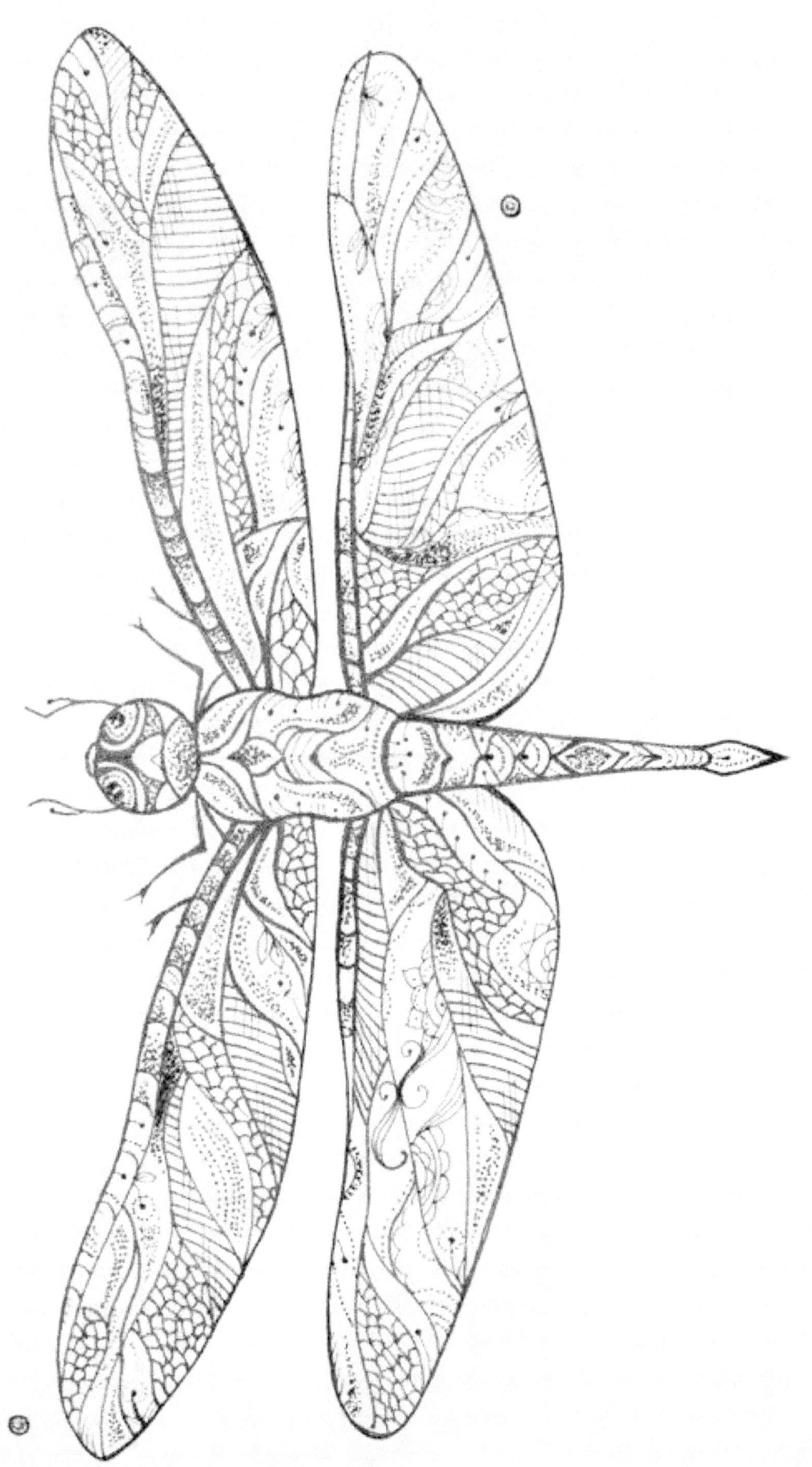

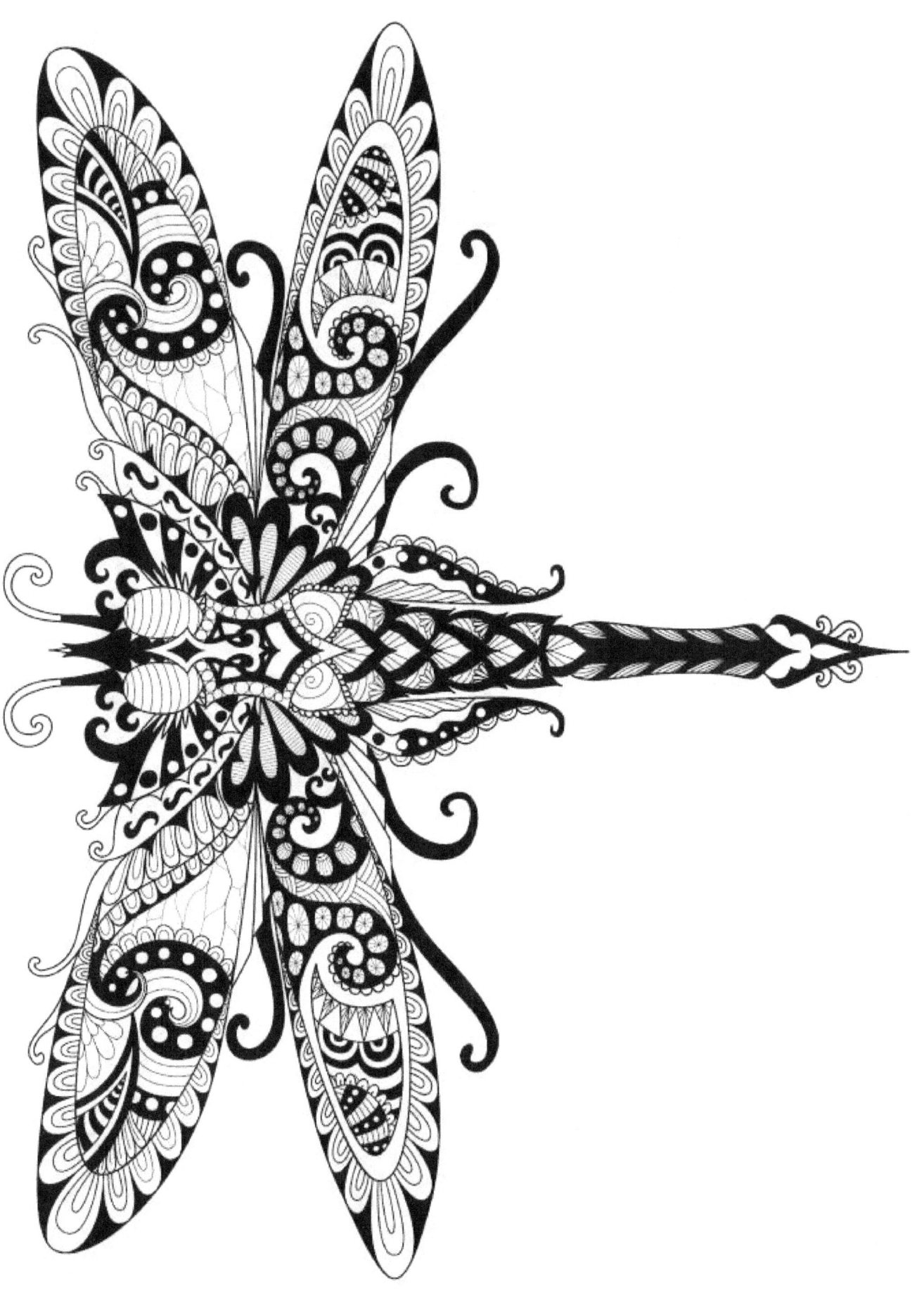

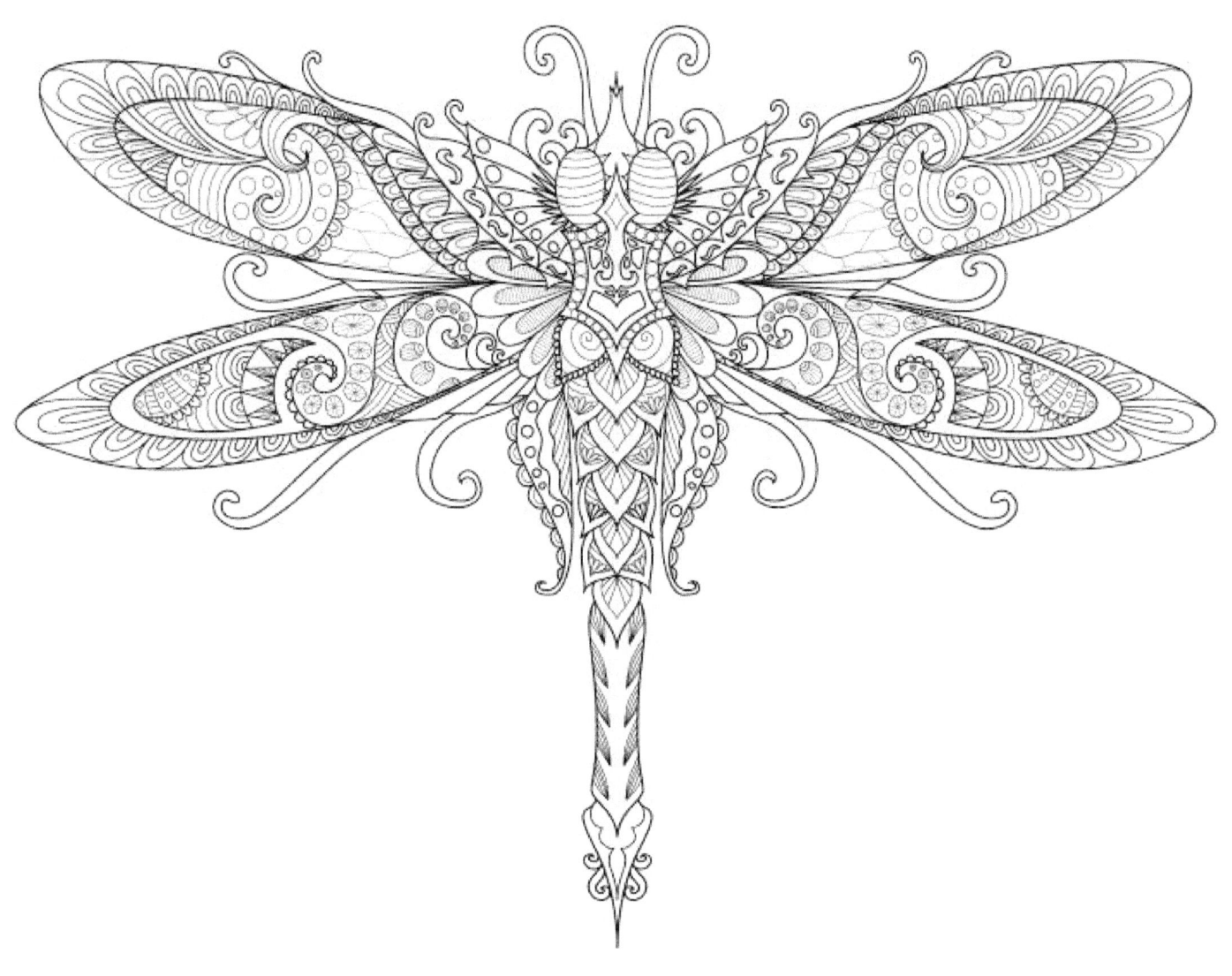

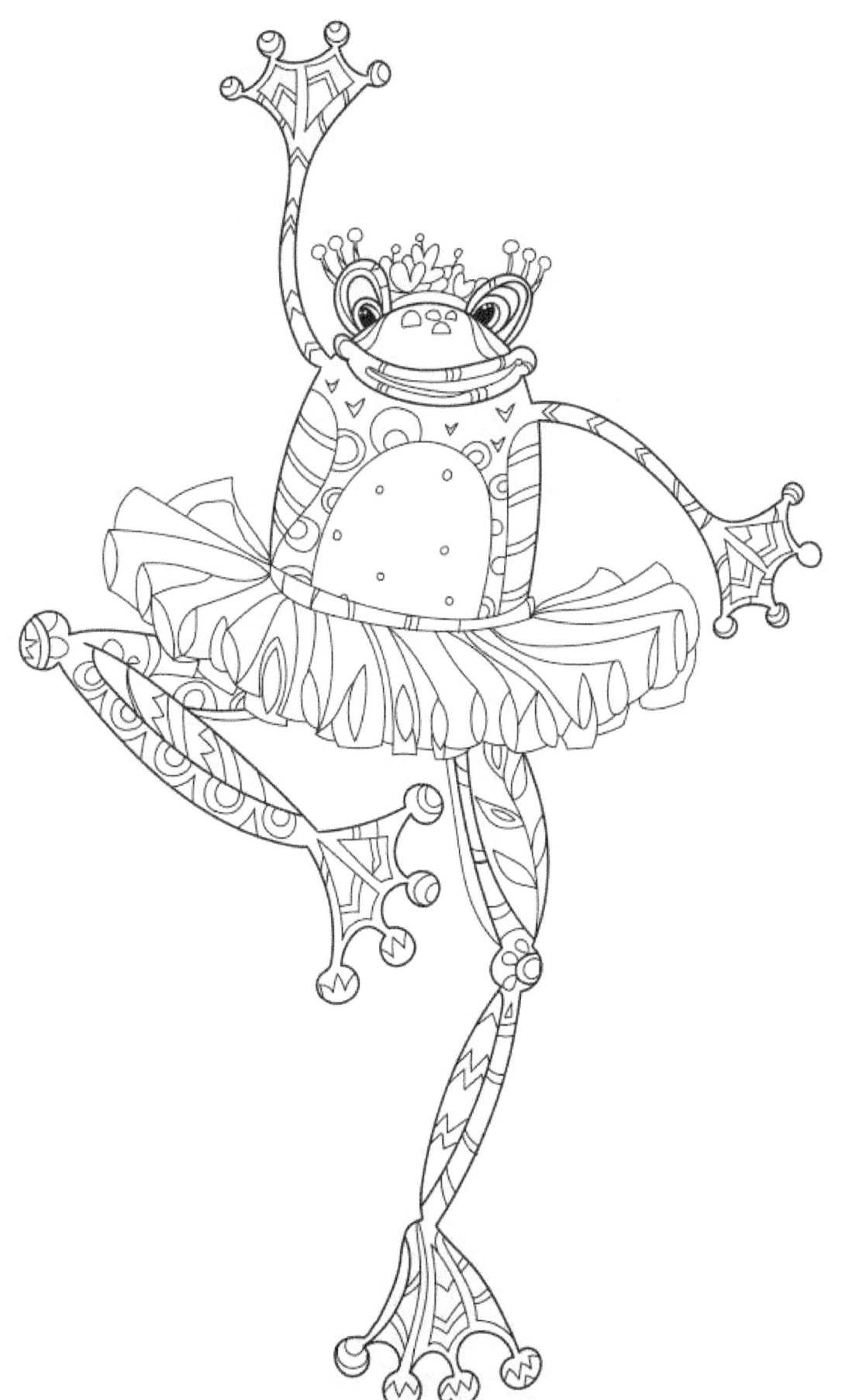

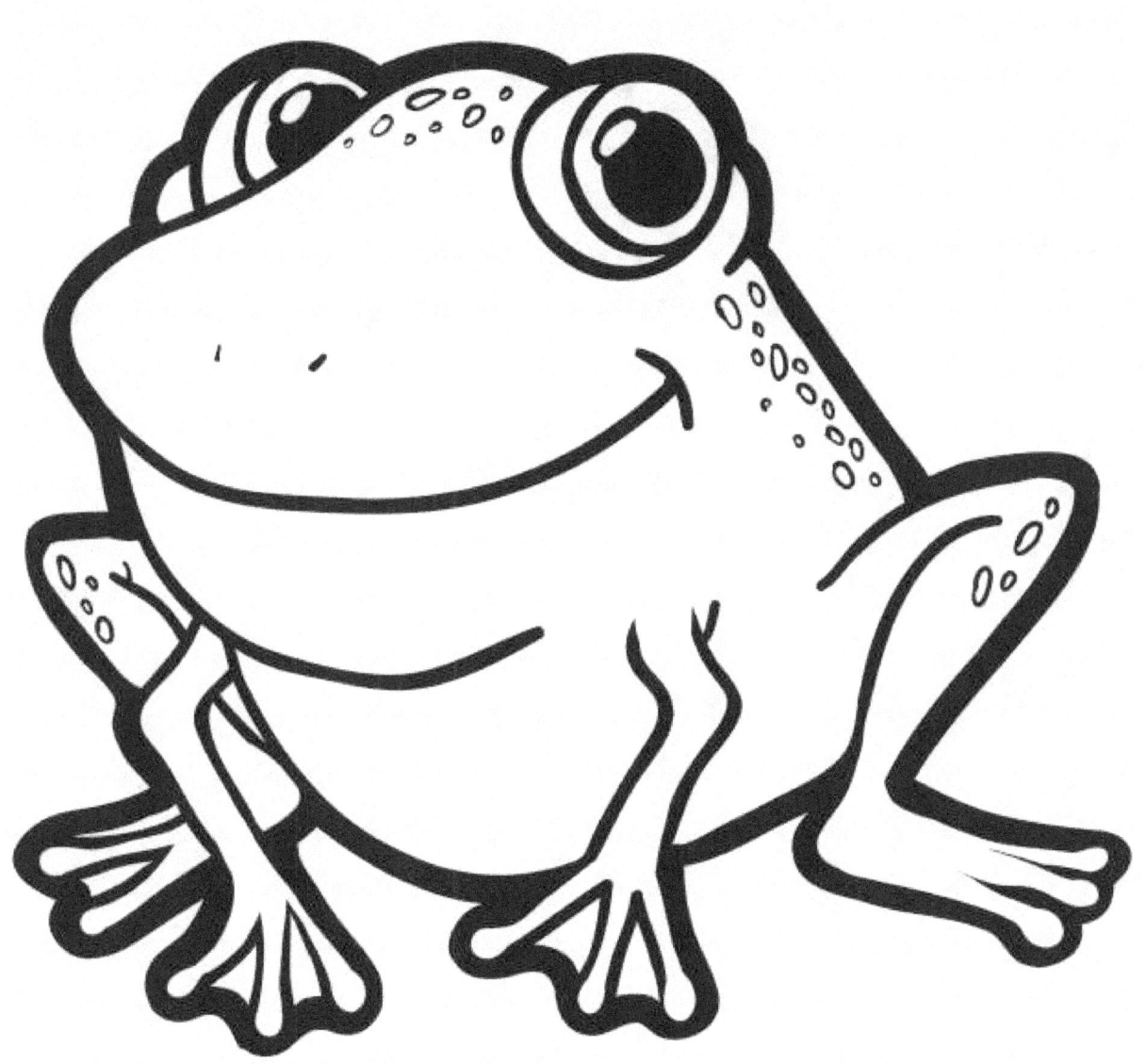

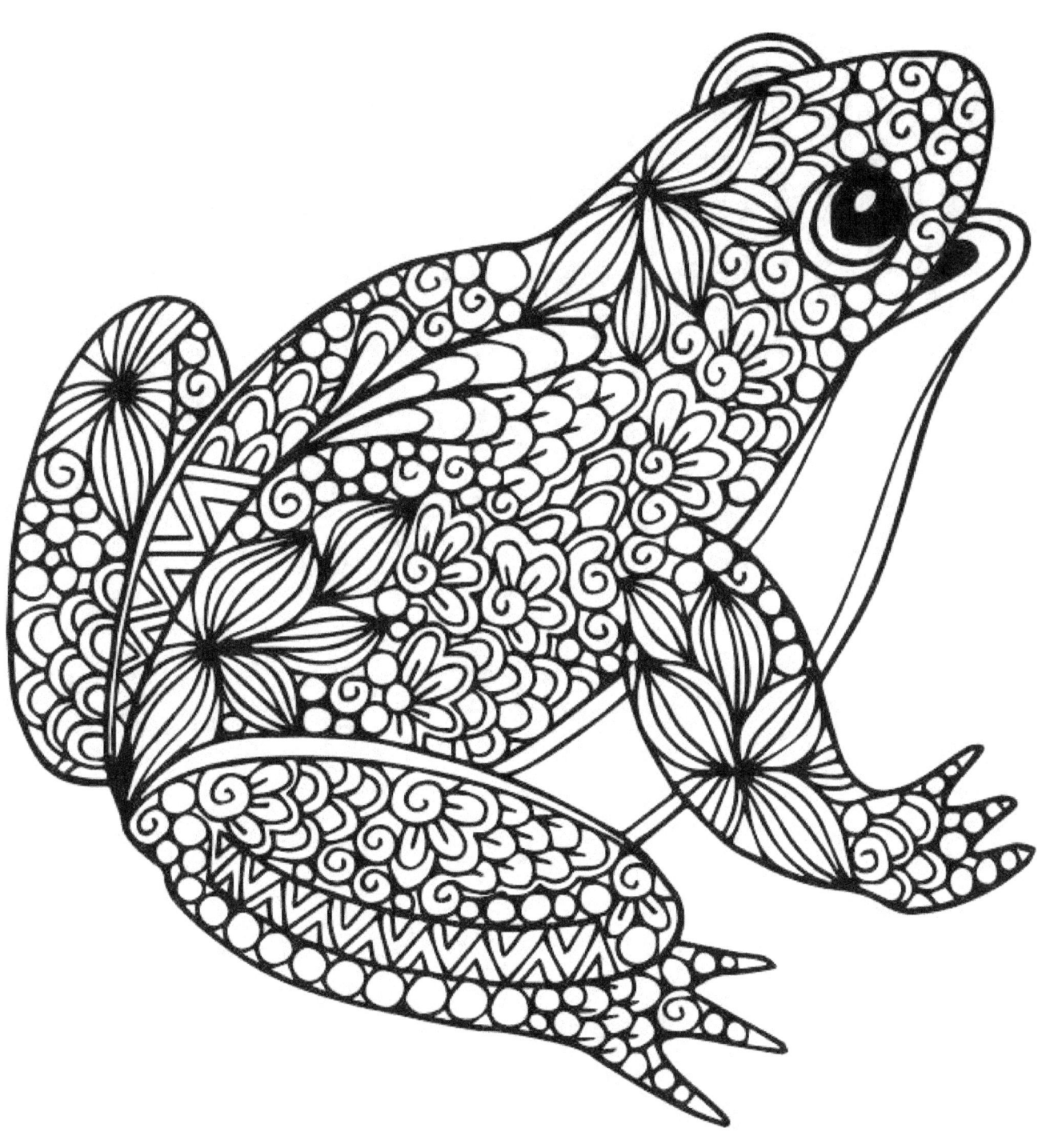

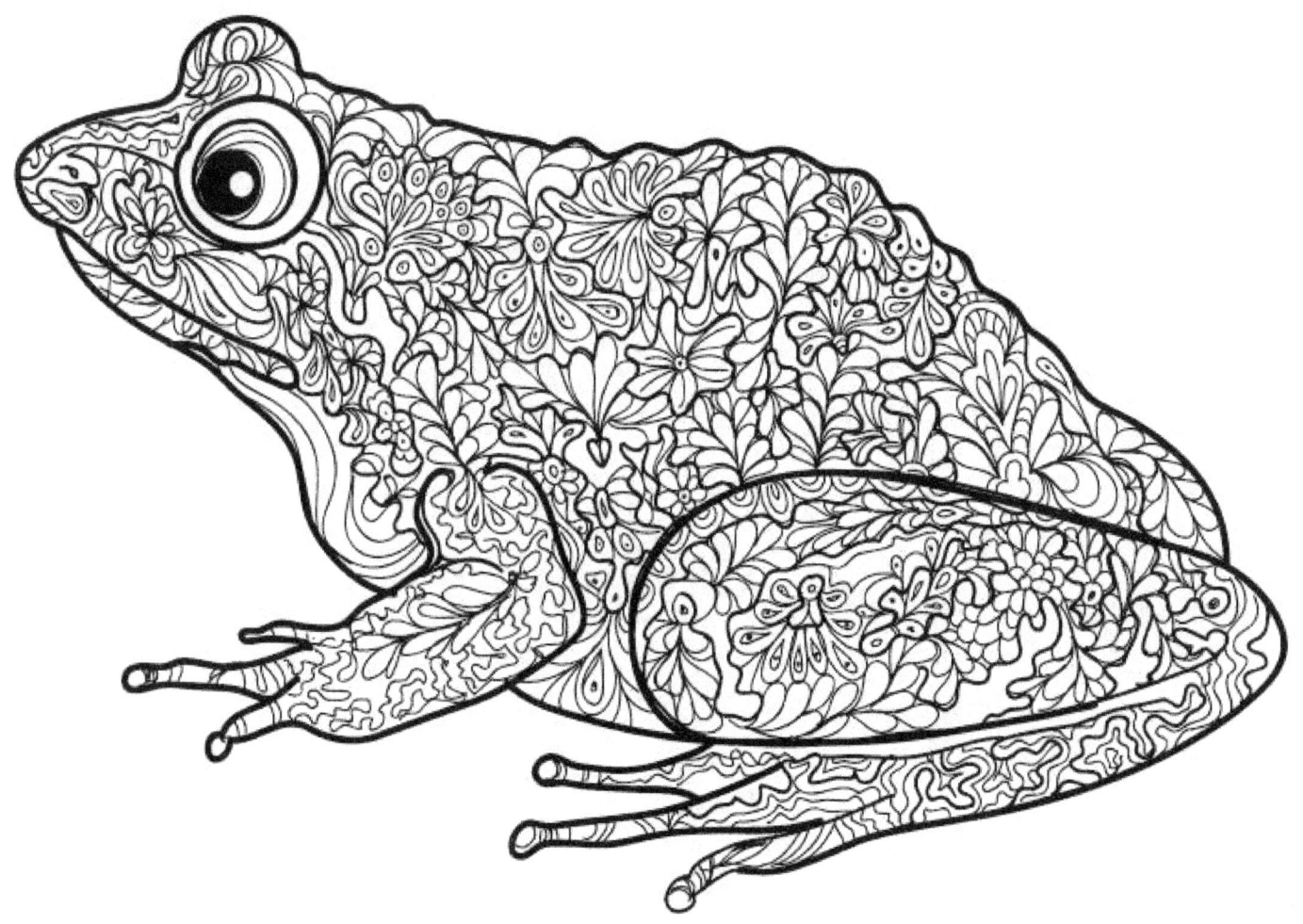

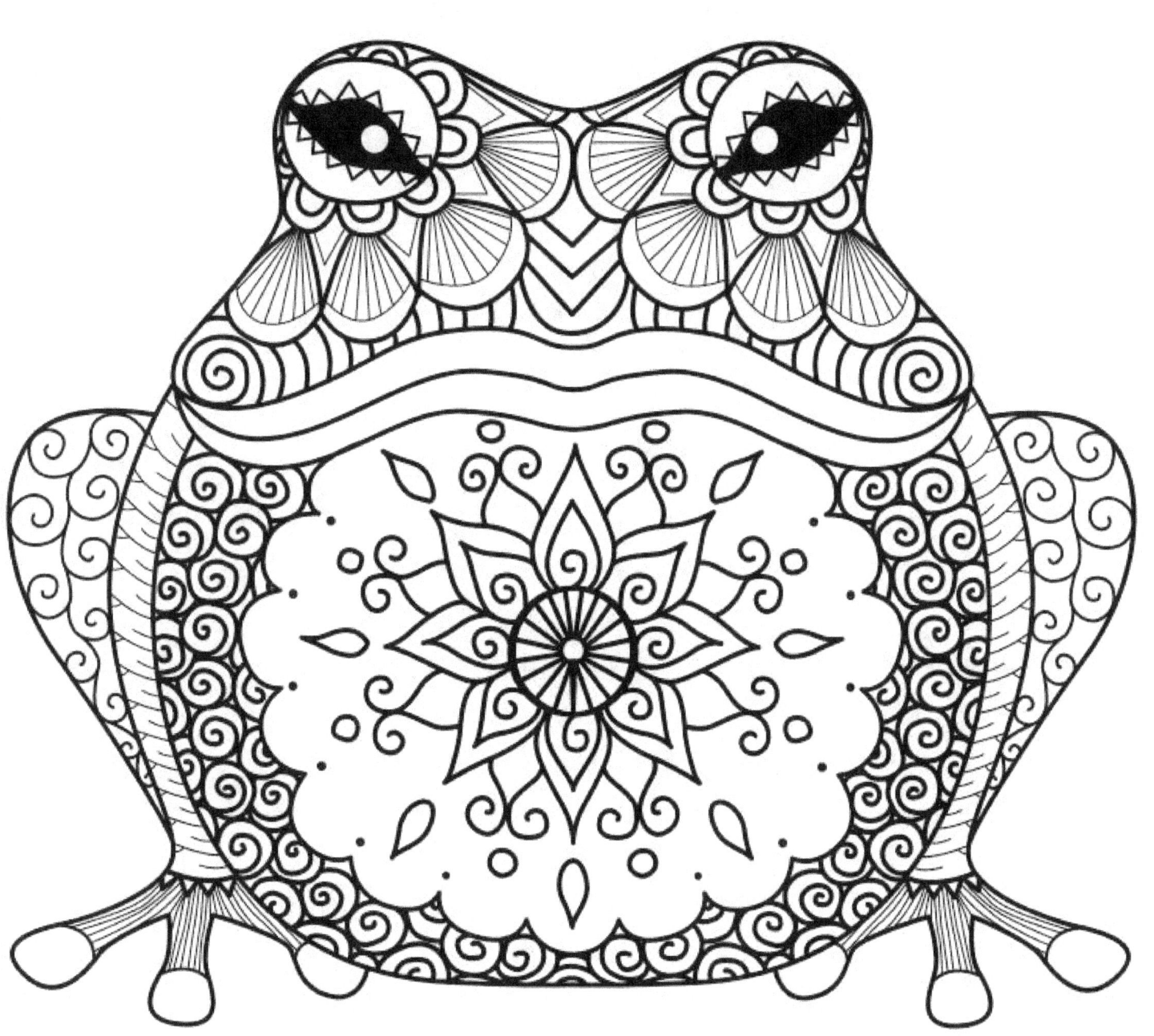

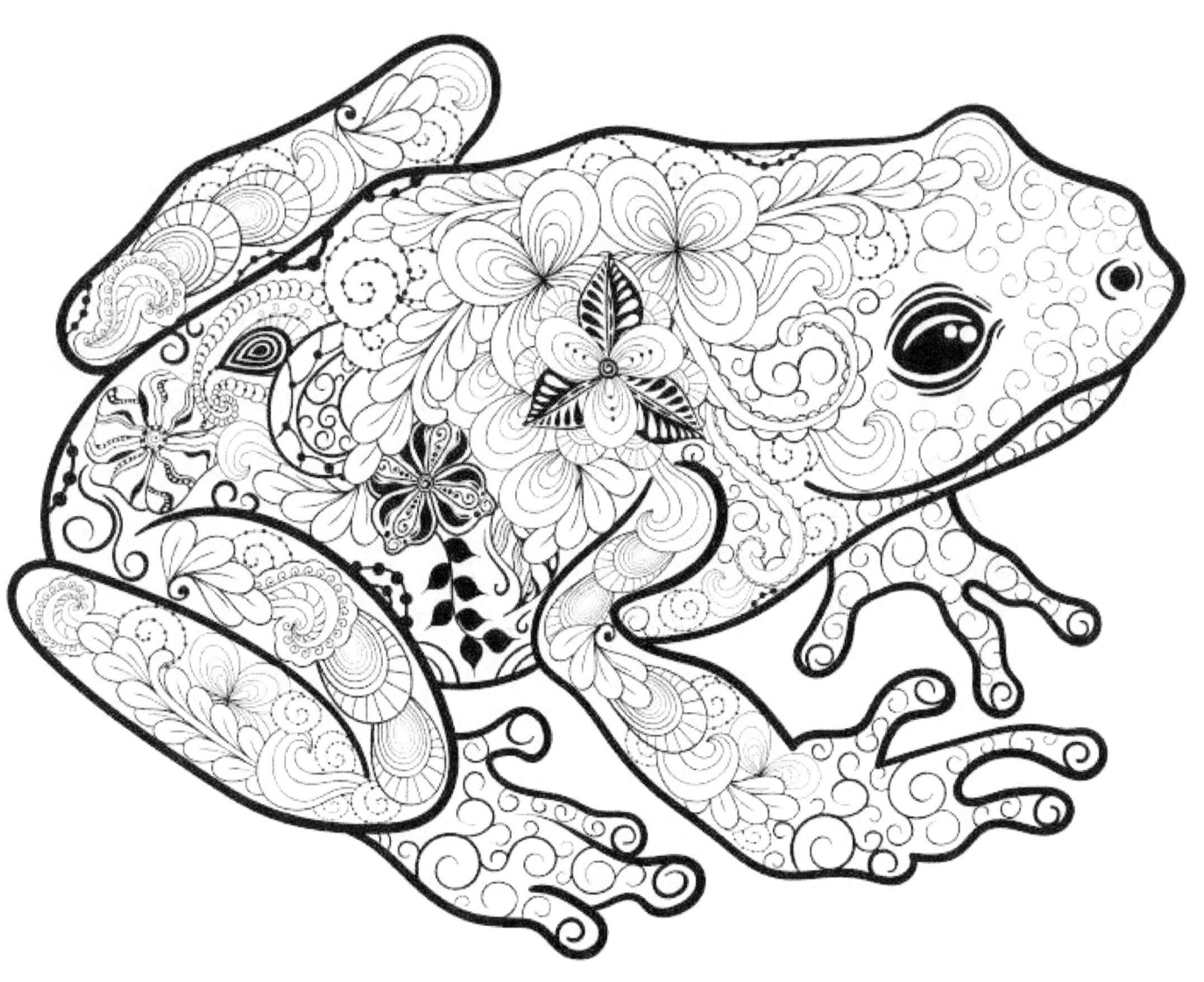

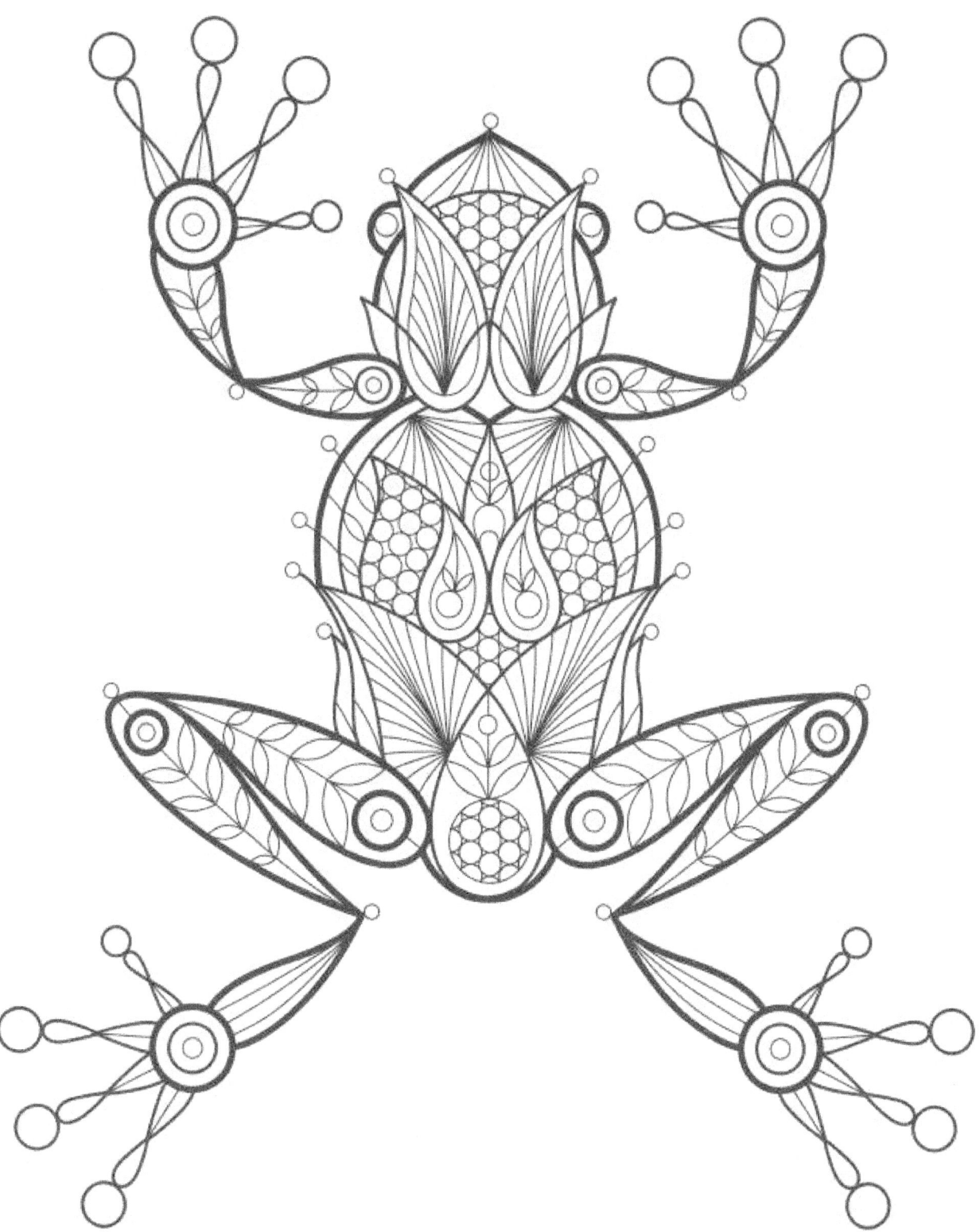

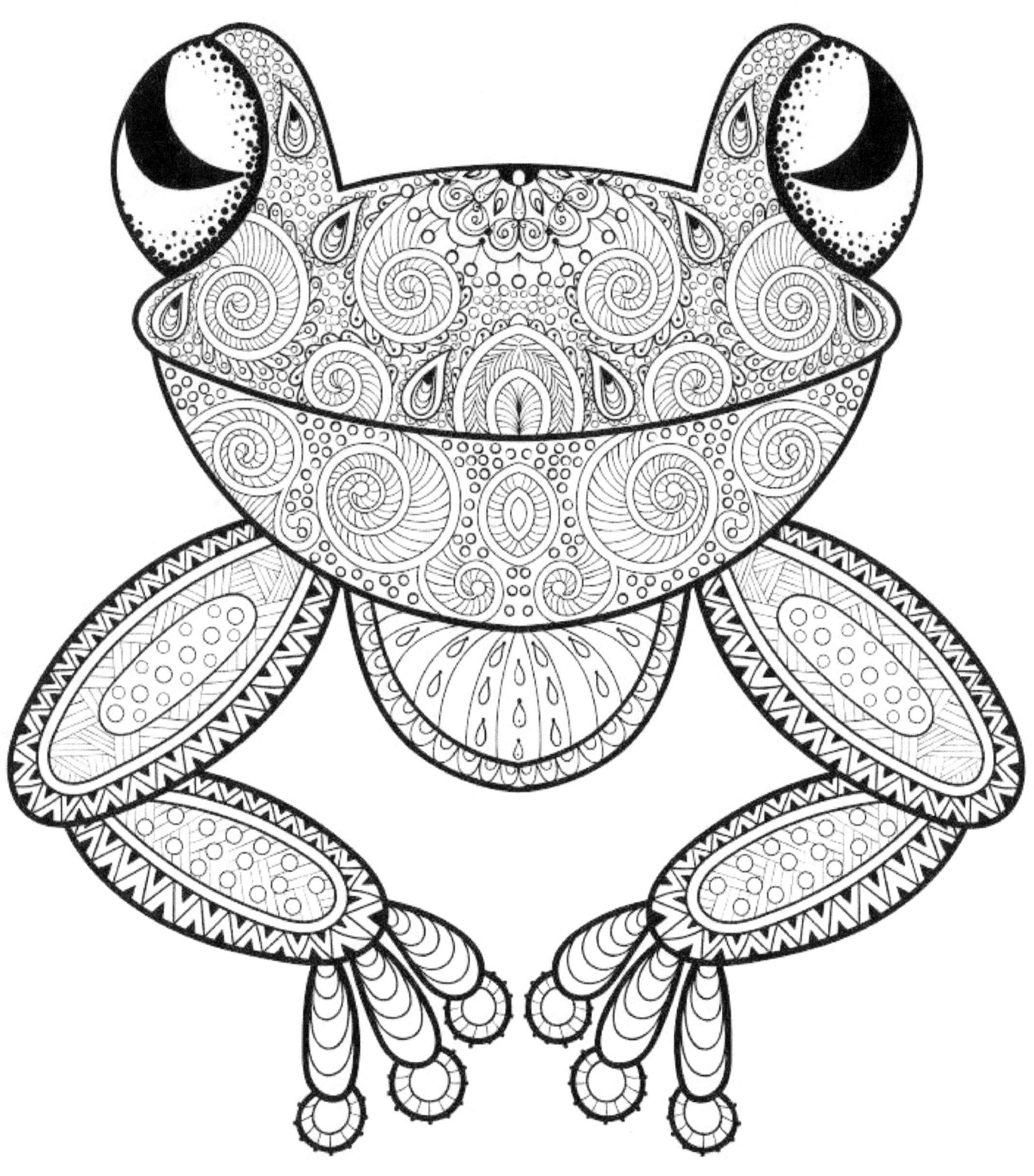

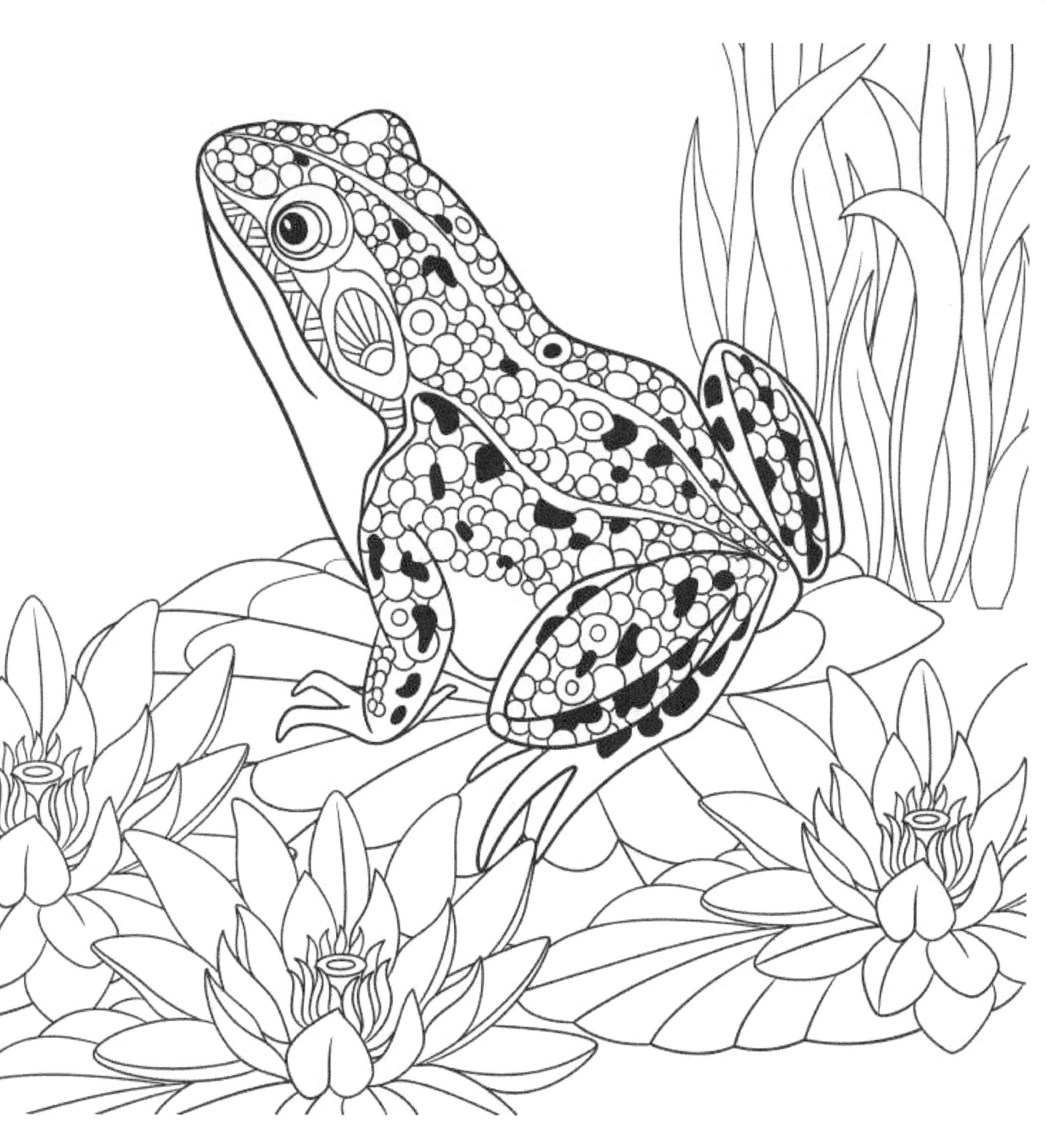

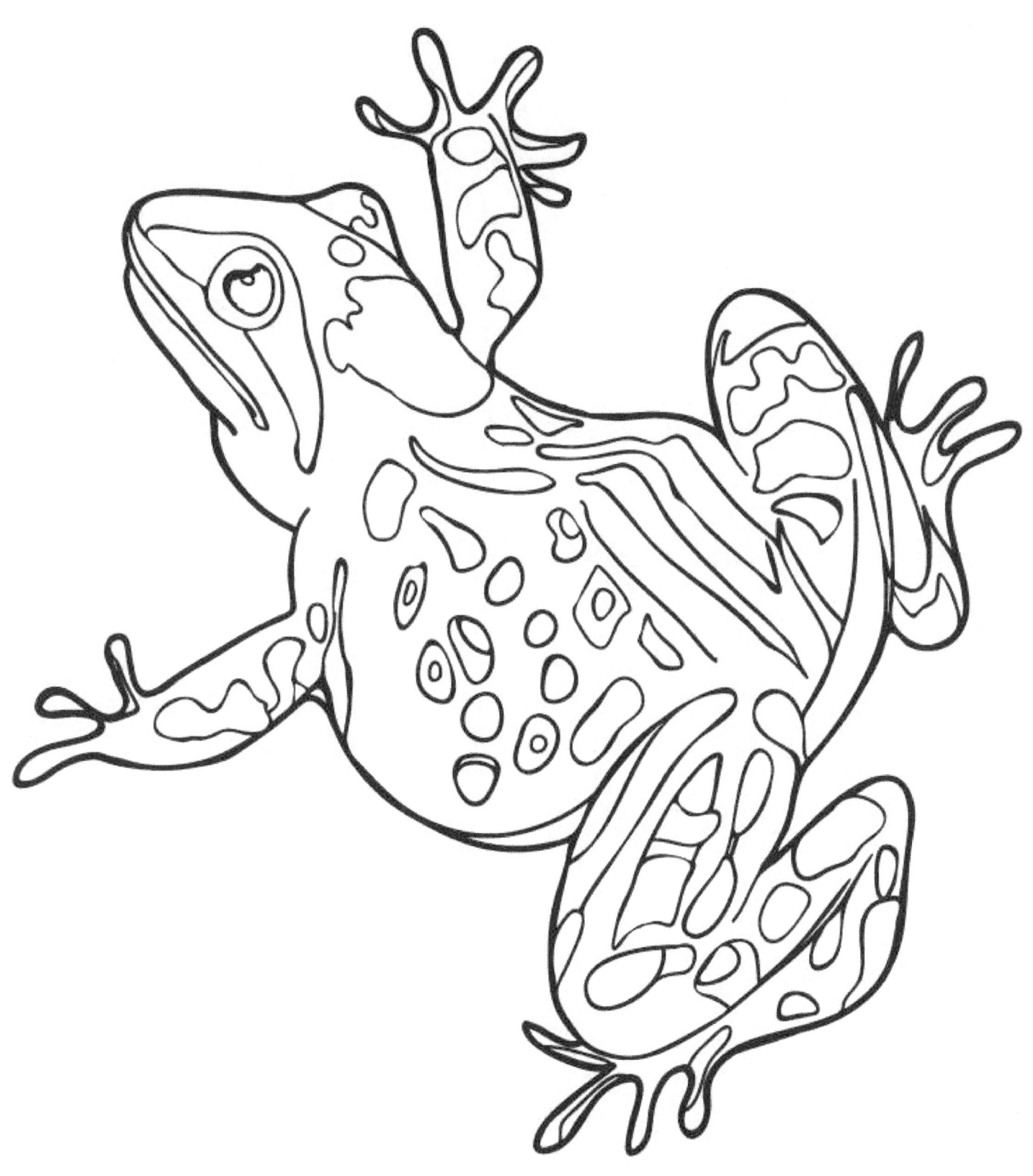

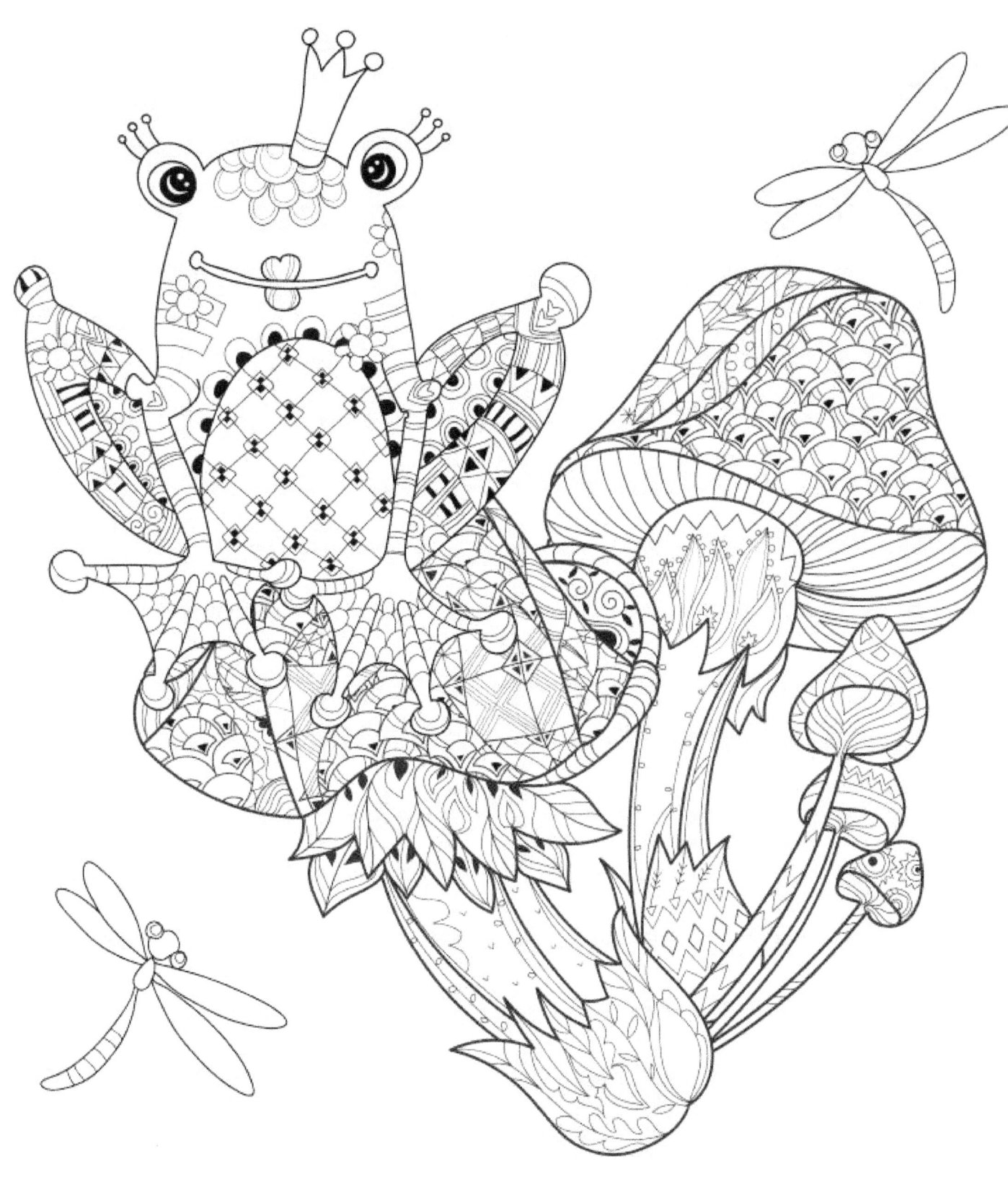

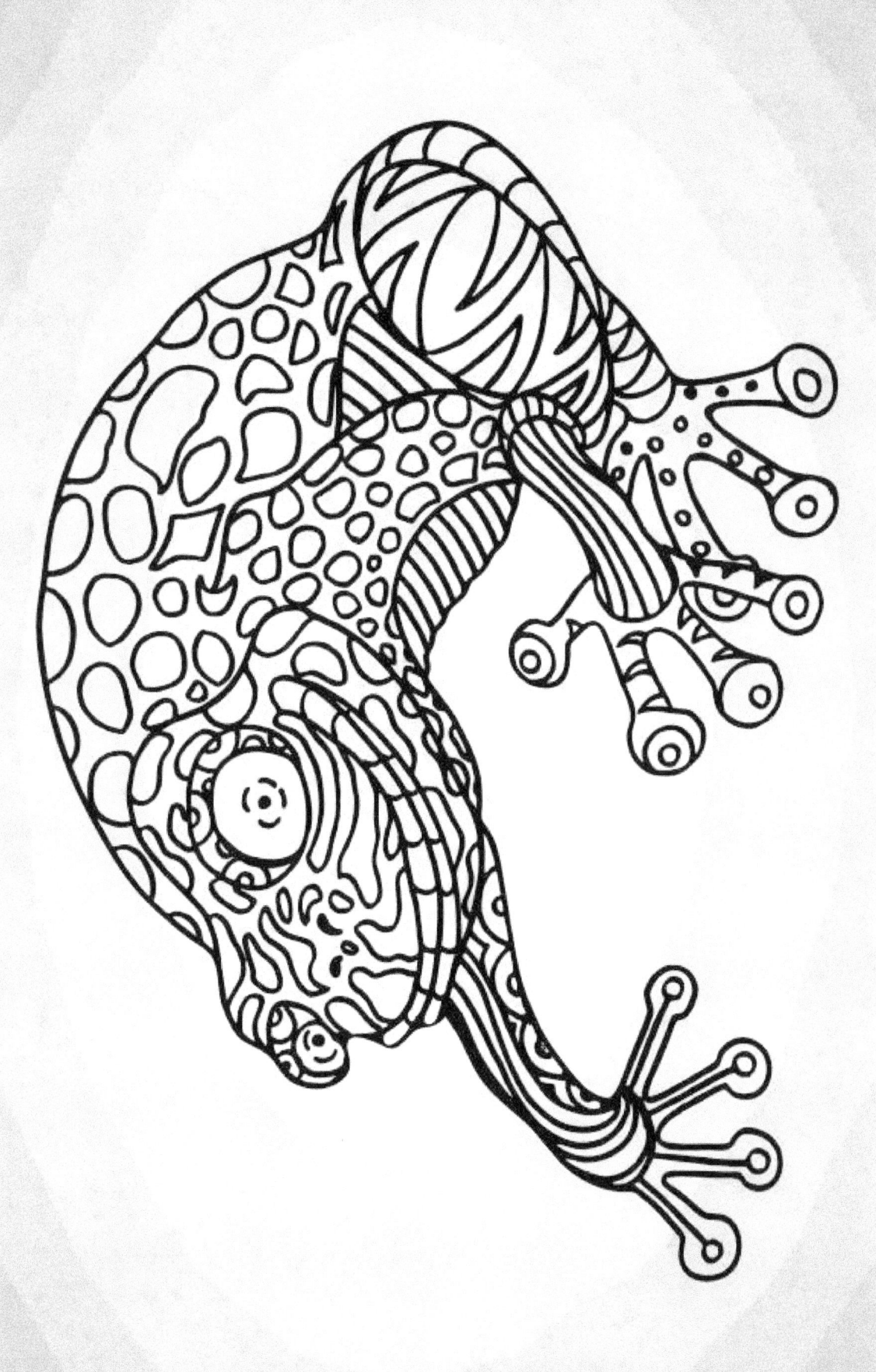

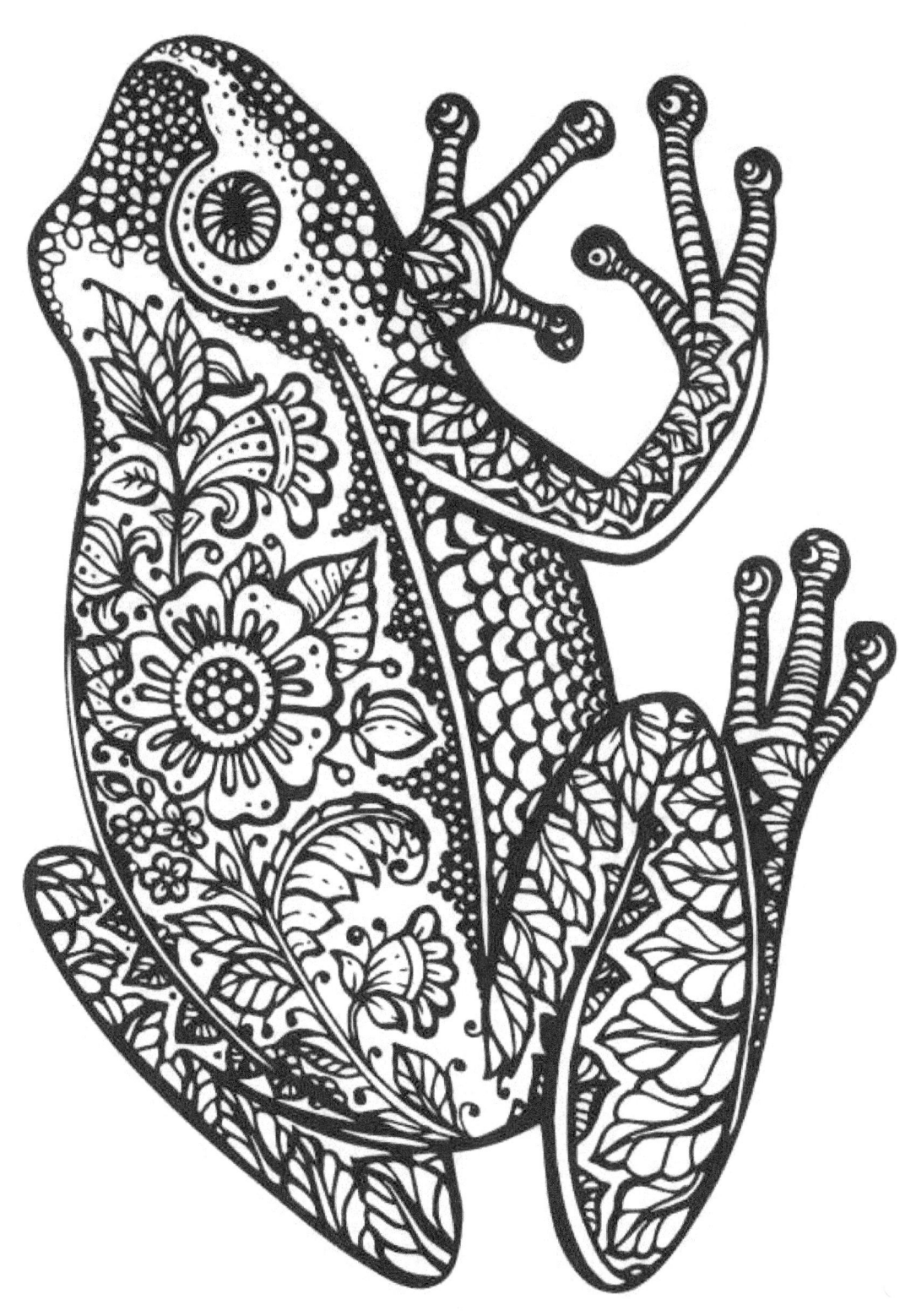

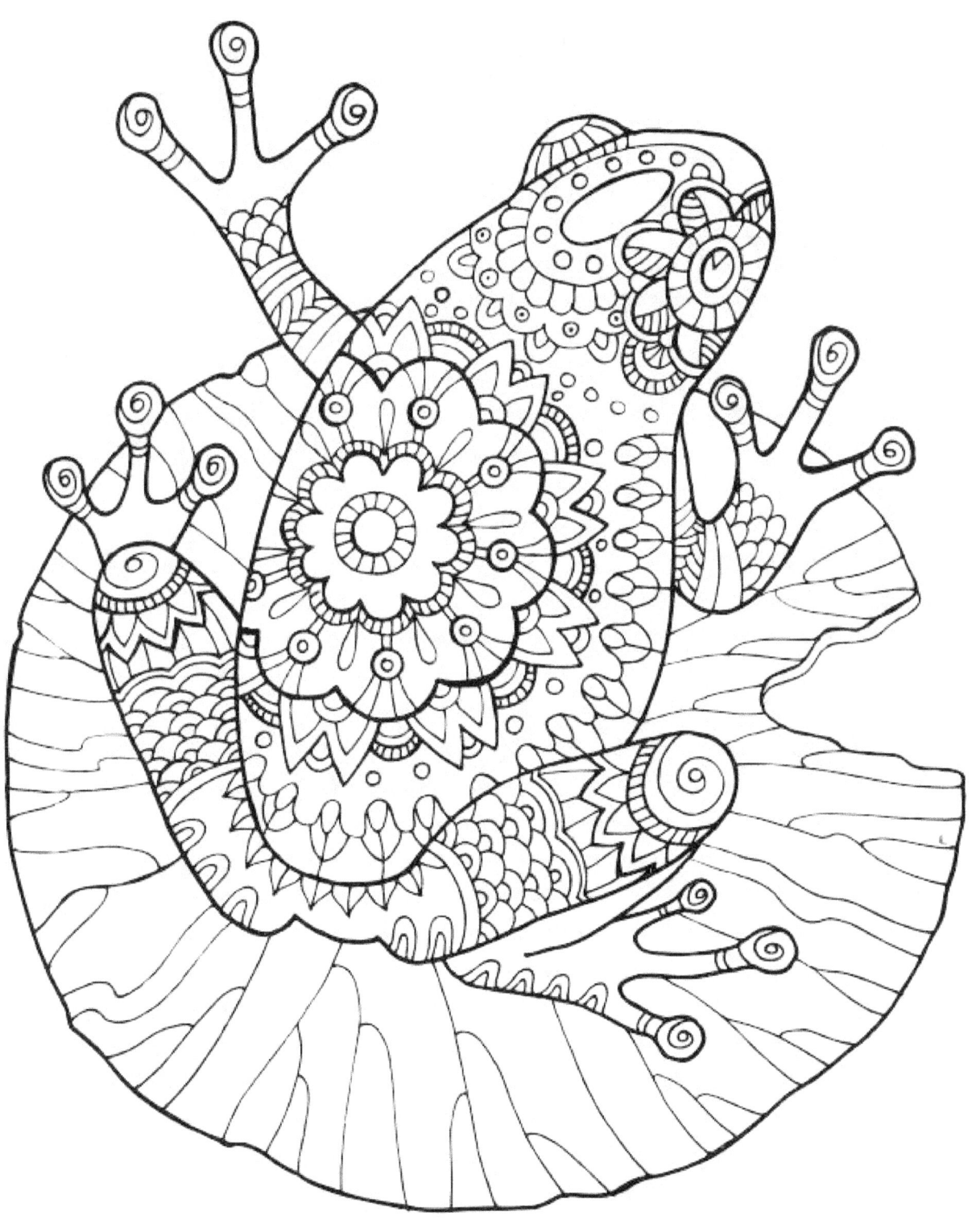

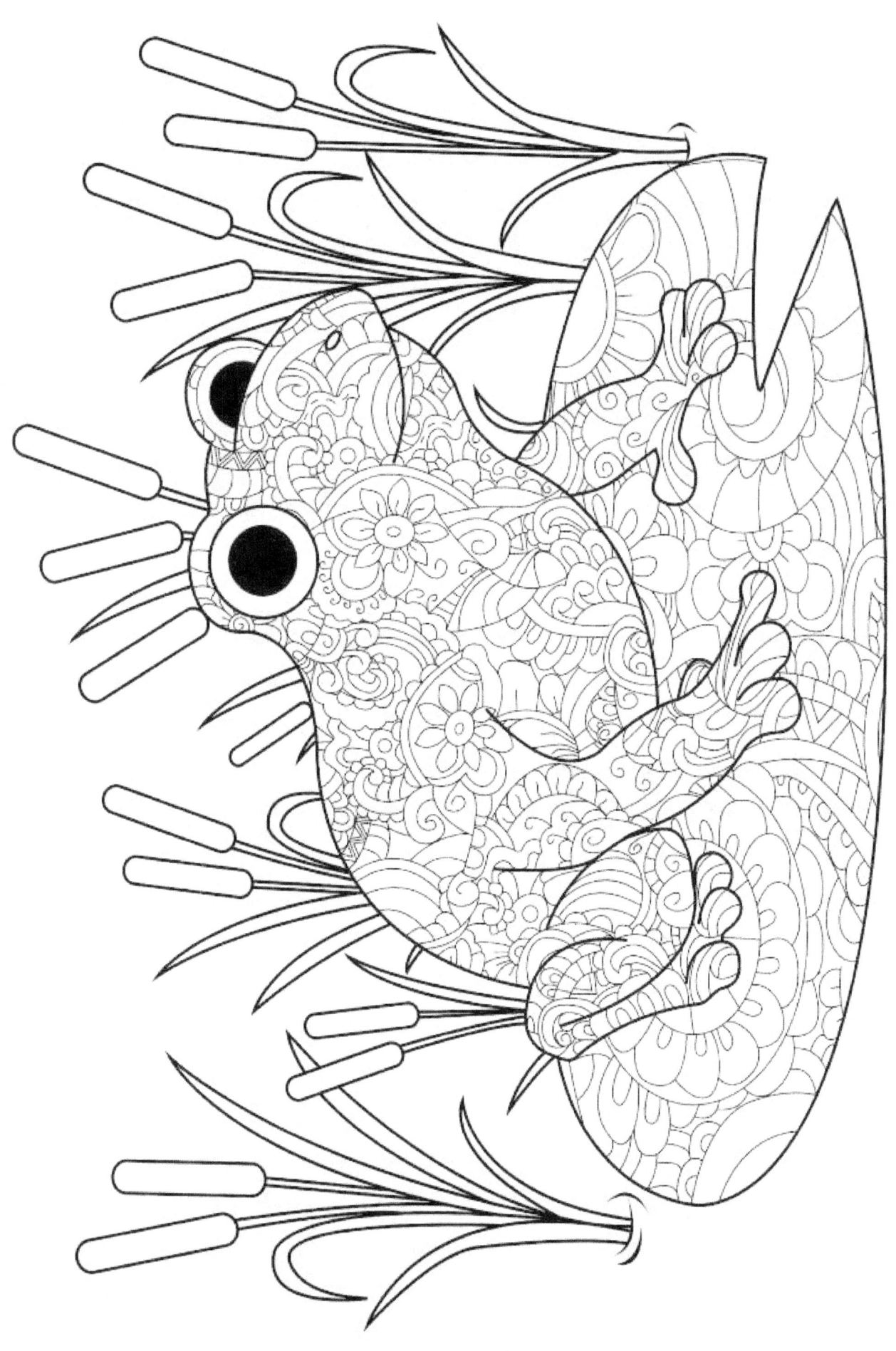

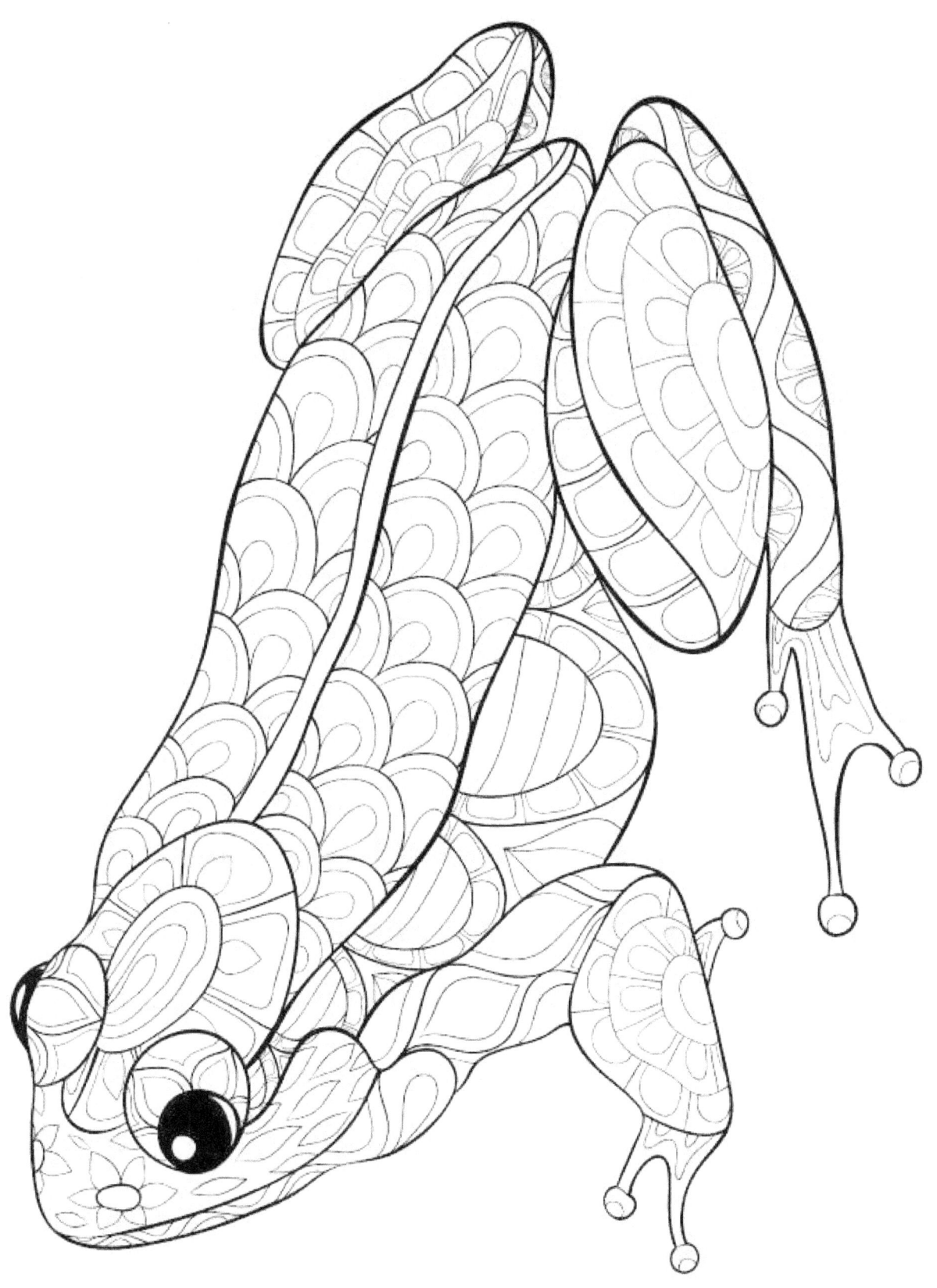

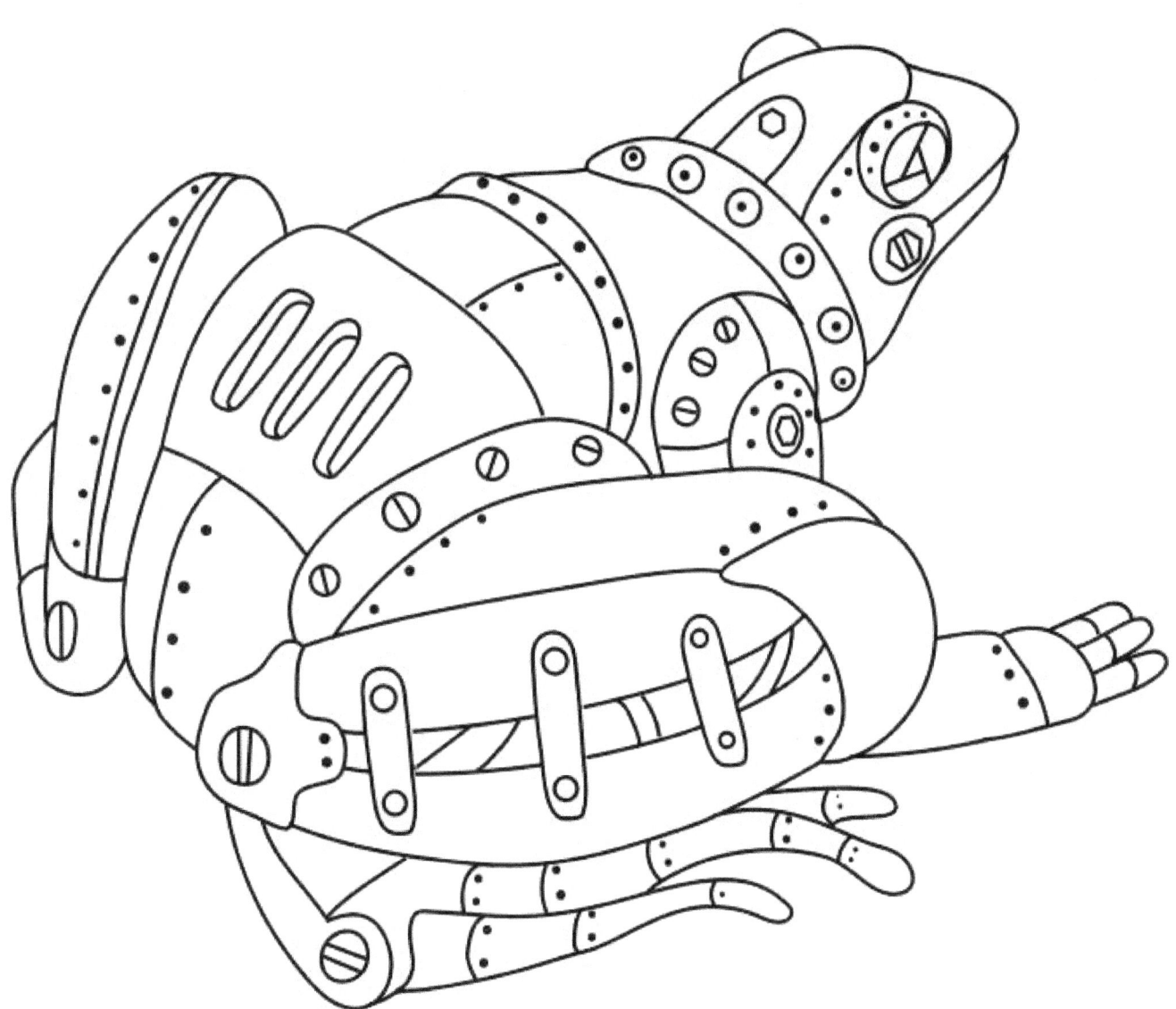

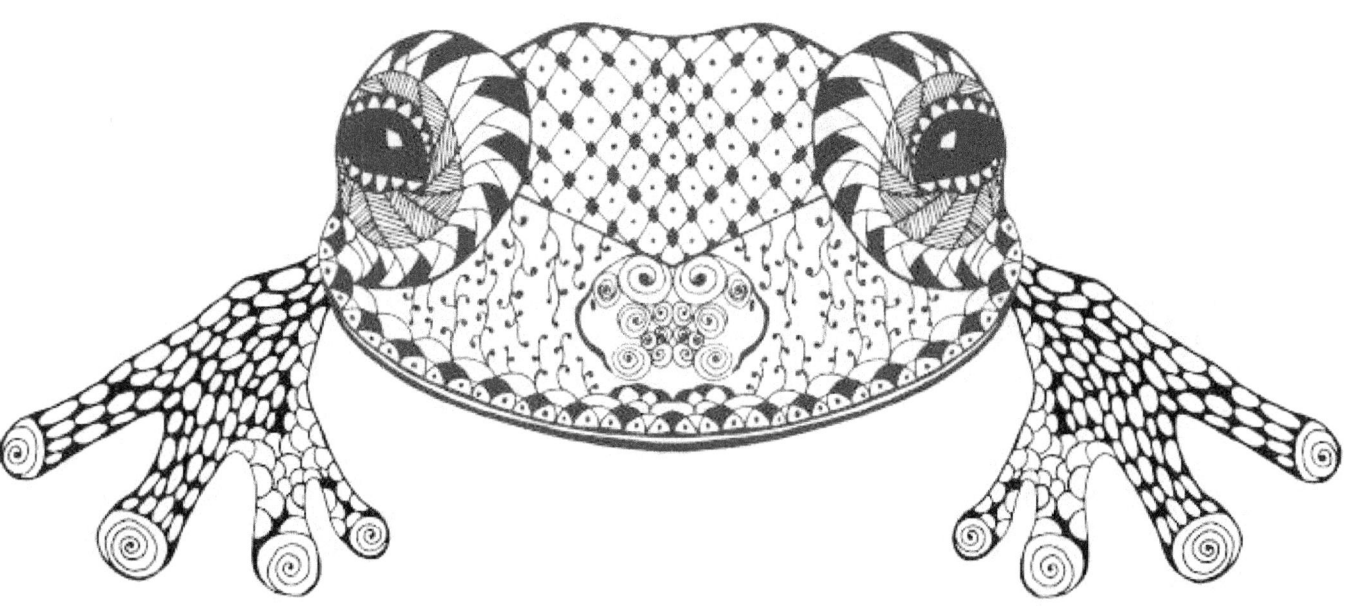

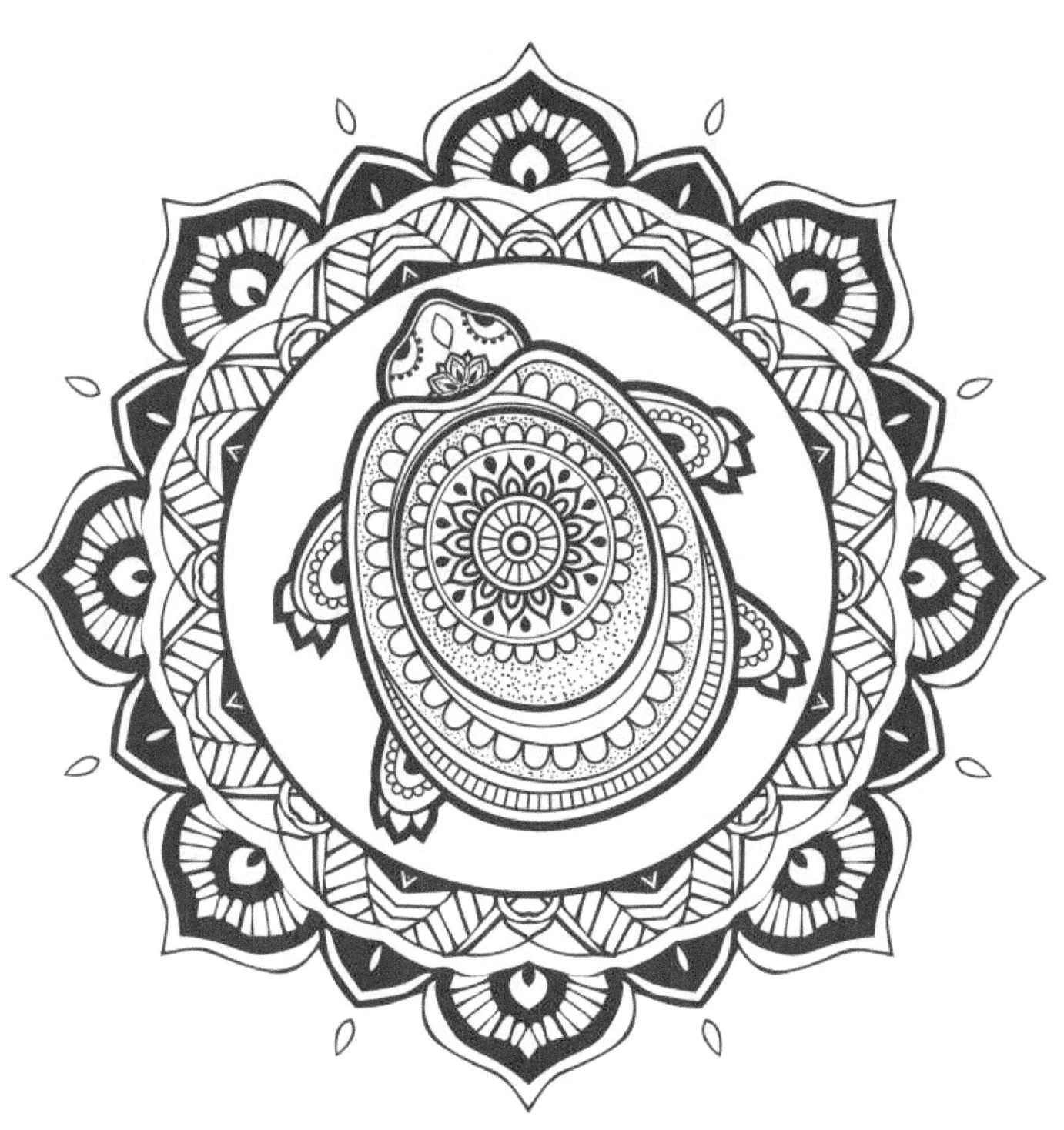

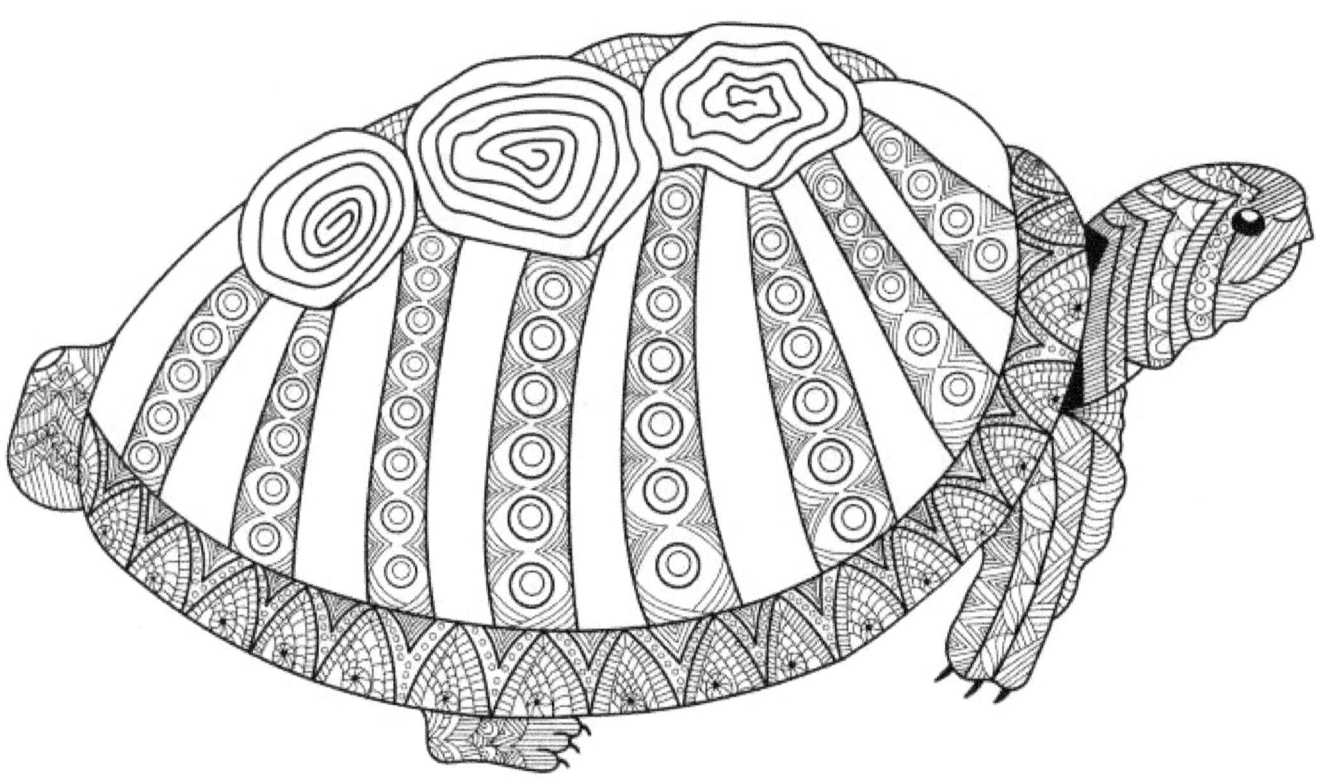

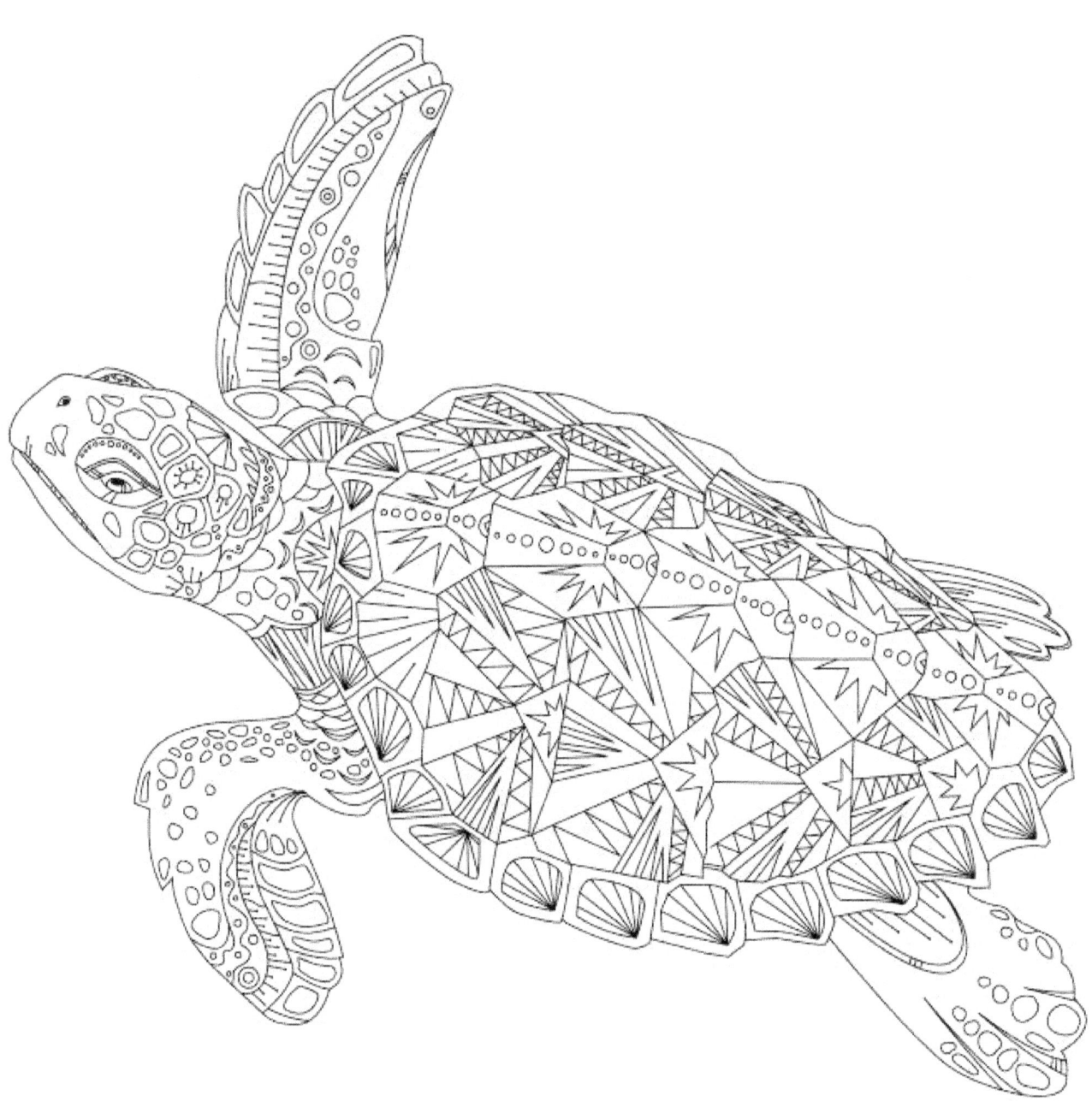

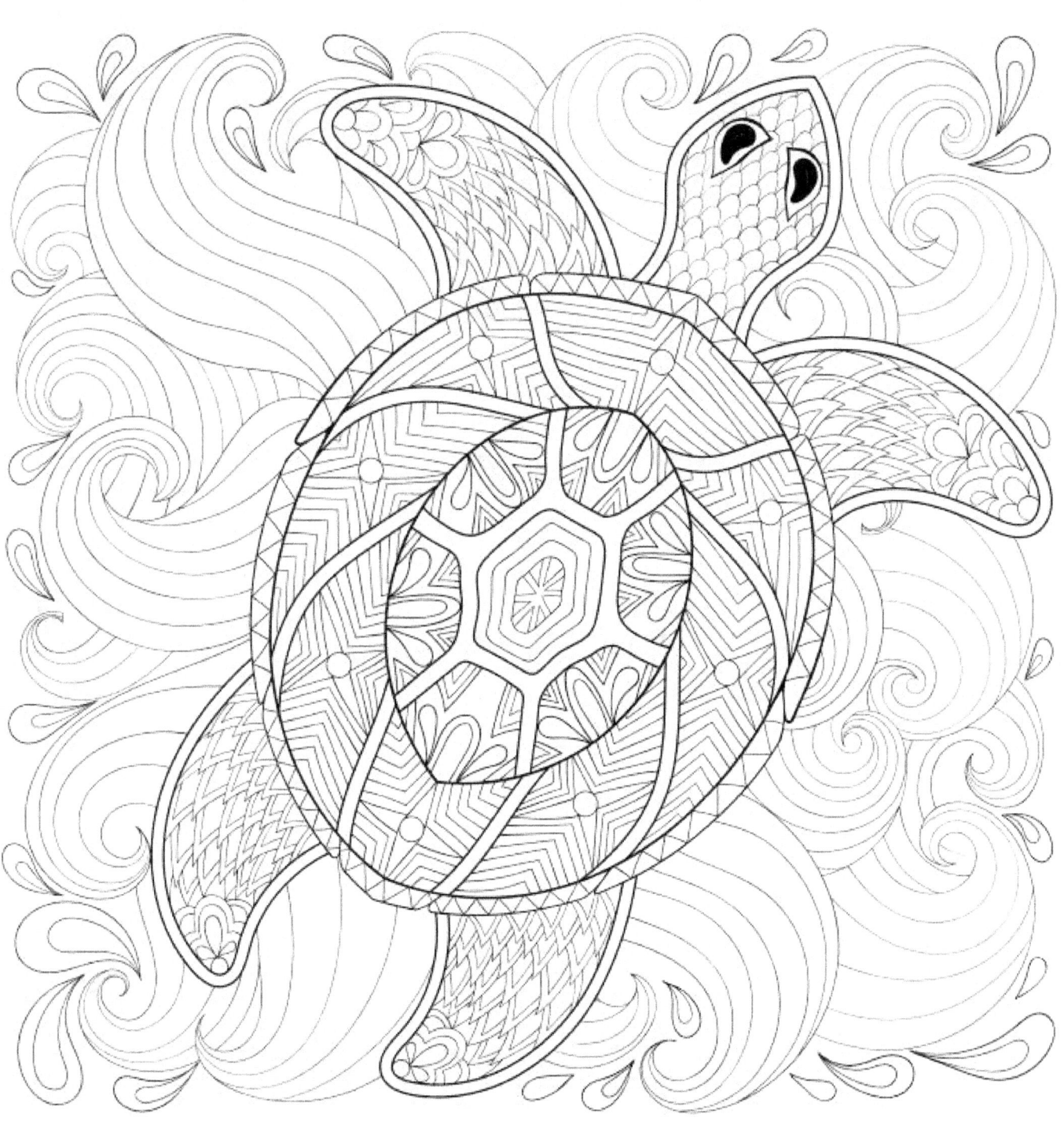

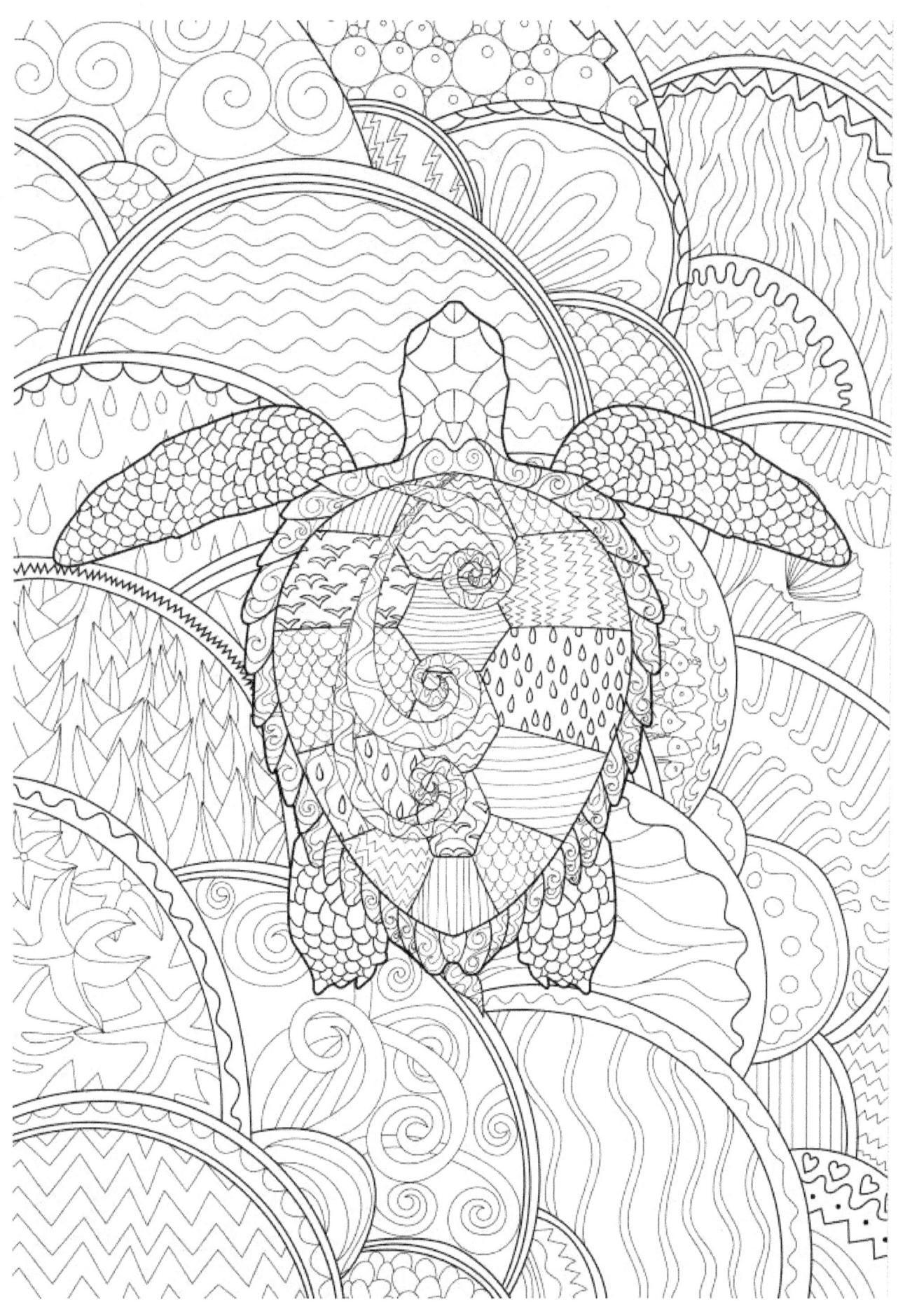

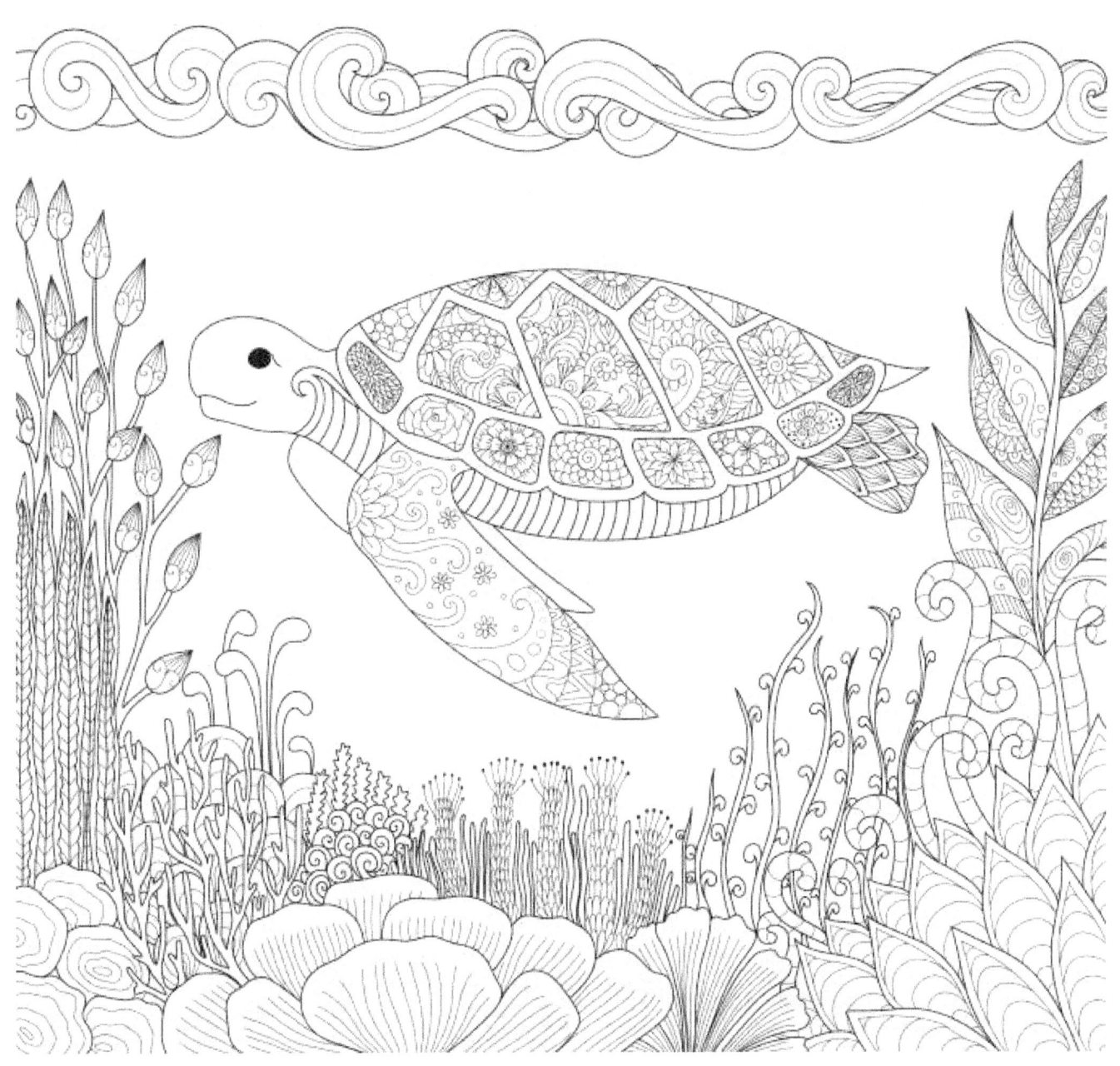

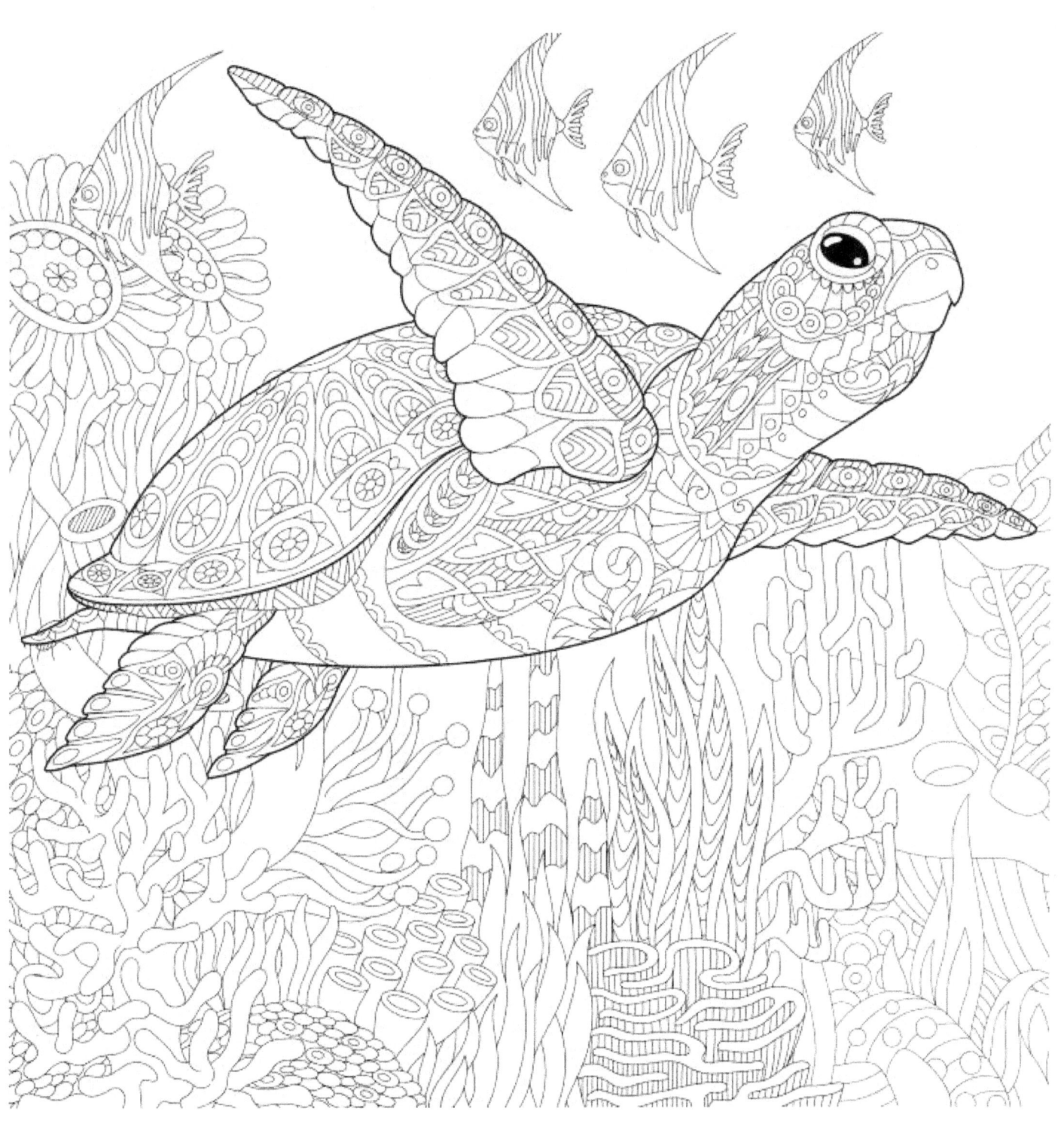

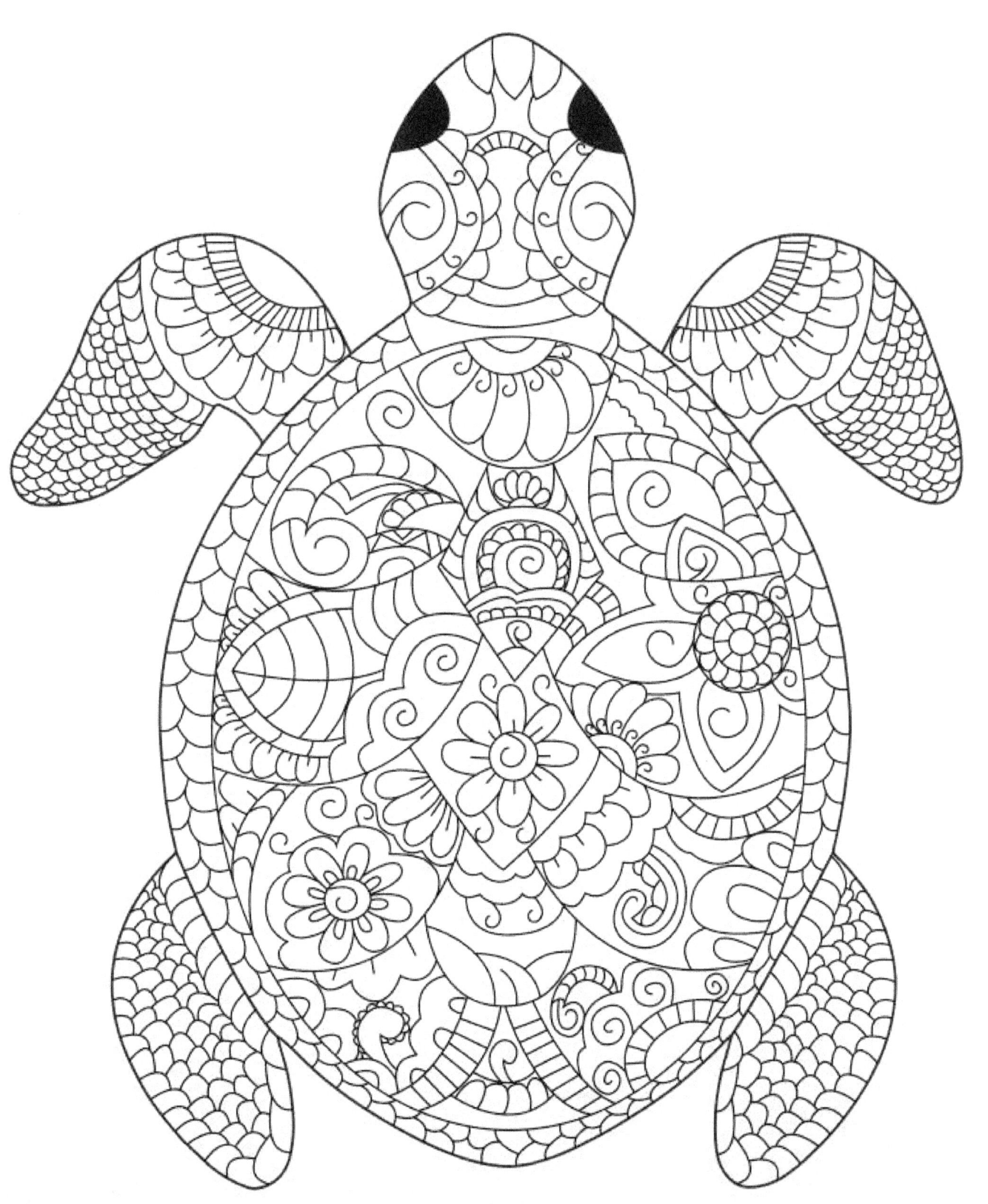

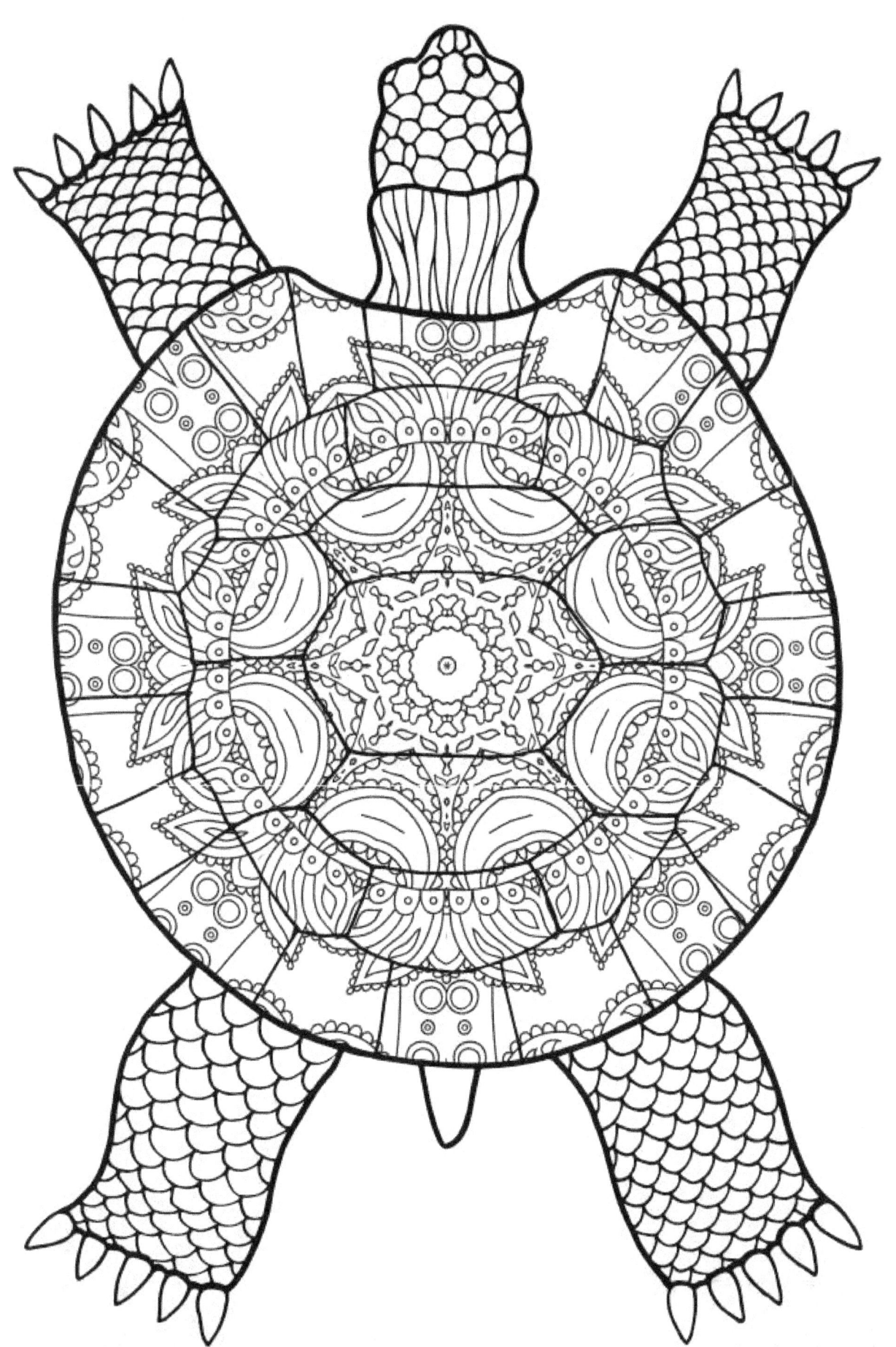

www.ingramcontent.com/pod-product-compliance
Lightning Source LLC
Chambersburg PA
CBHW082330220526
45470CB00008B/2459